WHEN YOU'RE
UP TO
YOUR

IN ALLIGATORS…

WHEN YOU'RE UP TO YOUR A S S IN ALLIGATORS...

More Urban Folklore from the Paperwork Empire

ALAN DUNDES

CARL R. PAGTER

Wayne State University Press   Detroit

92   91   90   89   88   2   3   4   5   6

Library of Congress Cataloging-in-Publication Data

When you're up to your ass in alligators—more urban
    folklore from the paperwork empire.

    1. Urban folklore—United States. 2. Office practice
—United States—Folklore. 3. Xerography—Folklore.
4. American wit and humor. 5. United States—Social life
and customs—1971-   . I. Dundes, Alan. II. Pagter,
Carl R., 1934-
GR105.W47 1987   817'.54'080321732   87-3056
ISBN 0-8143-1866-5
ISBN 0-8143-1867-3 (pbk.)

Grateful acknowledgment is made to the *Journal of Applied Behavior Analysis*
(No. 3 [Fall, 1974]: 497) for permission to reprint "The Unsuccessful Self-
Treatment of a Case of 'Writer's Block.'" The authors of this volume are
otherwise unaware of any known author of any of the items appearing in this
volume. If there was an original author, the name has disappeared in the office-
copier transmission process.

Contents

Those Cards and Letters   67

The Writing on the Walls: Notices, Mottoes, and Awards   90

Parity for Parody   234

Conclusions   268

Preface

This second collaboration between a professor of folklore and an attorney whose avocation is folksinging would not have been possible without the assistance of many students, colleagues, and friends who generously shared with us examples of office copier folklore in their possession. Although many of the items we received were duplicates of materials that had already appeared in our first volume, many others helped confirm the traditionality of items we had collected earlier but had not included in the first volume. Some of the items were new to us. We would like to thank all those who took the time to send us examples of urban folklore. In large measure they made this compilation possible.

We would like to convey our appreciation to all the following and we apologize to any whose names we may have inadvertently omitted. James B. Adams, Bruce Bauer, Paul Berkstresser, Gary Bogue, Lars Bourne, Tom Bowdle, Ken Bradshaw, Jan Brunvand, Dick Corten, Judie Cox, Henry E. Cunningham, Hal T. Curtis, Ken Dachman, Mandalit del Barco, Comerlis Delaney, Robert P. Dempsey, James Diestel, Scott Dunham, Debra Eglit, Hanne Eilers, Sheryl A. Ernest, Penelope Foster, Robert Friedman, John Funke, Burney Garelick, Victoria George, Donna Goldstein, Joe Goldstein, Gus and Judy Greden, Thomas D. Hall, Lee Haring, Jill Heenan, Julia Hernandez, Joe Hickerson, Frank Hoffmann, Elizabeth Hofmayer, Fran Holliday, William Holt, Mary Hoole, Jane Hosier, Bob Howard, David Hunn, Diana Hunt, Mike Hutchinson, Mark Hypnar, Vicki Inger, Moira Jackson, Judi Jacobs, John Johnson, Anna Jones, James D. Kaufman, Kristine Keller, Susan Kerstein, Ian Keye, Jan Kidd, Barbara Kirshenblatt-Gimblett, Patricia Kramer, Anne Leong, Brian Lesnansky, Monica Ley, Kathryne Lindberg, W. J. Lindgren, Jay J. London, Peter Lovett, Carol

McBride, Neil McCallum, Marjorie McCants, Alexandra McEwen, Lindy McGlaughlin, John McKibben, Wayne McNabb, John Madden, Micaela di Leonardo Magowan, R. L. Maier, Kathy Mallory, Sandra Manning, Francine Marshall, Mary Marzotto, Patricia Mason, Janet Matz, Esther May, Dan Melia, Phil Mikelson, Susan Montagne, Jo Anne Morrow, Mabel Muller, Karen Nessen, Jack Newman, Michael Nisley, Betsy Noble, Frank Norick, Bill O'Keefe, Emmett O'Neill, B. E. Olsen, Barbara O'Rand, Julie Pattillo, Barbara Papini, Jose Pereira, Michael Poniatowski, Joseph Powers, Michael Preston, Tom Rees, C. W. Reese, Amy L. Renalds, Nancy Ripsteen, Wendy Rose, Barbara Ruemler, John Sandy, Kris Scammell, Barbara Scheifler, Larry A. Schroeder, Richard Schroeder, Ted Schucat, Kathryn Shopler, Barbara Jade Sironen, Frank Smalley, Norman D. Stevens, Charles W. Stevenson, Mark Taxy, Charles Tips, Judy Torrison, Harriet Tropp, M. J. Tyler, Allen Vegotsky, Karen Werner, Les Whitaker, Robert L. White, John Wooddell, Vicki L. Wong, Judith Young, Mary E. Zanolli, Mozell Zarit, and Rosemary Zumwalt.

Among the persons to whom we are indebted are several who had truly substantial collections of urban folklore, which they kindly made available to us. We should therefore like to offer special thanks to Michael E. Bell, Chick Berkstresser, Jess Burch, Emily D. Copenhaver, James Drahos, David Evans, Allene Fernandez, Garmen Gutierrez, Sue Hicks, Anne Koch, Wally Koenig, Ron Mesing, Eileen O'Hara, Curtis W. Shirley, Peter Tamony, and Sue Williams. We are particularly grateful to Nancy Ridenour not only for sharing her major collection of urban folklore with us, but also for her considerable expertise in this area.

We also owe a great deal to the Institute for Sex Research (ISR), known popularly as the Kinsey Institute, at Indiana University. This is one of the few places in the United States where one can find archival holdings of the type of material contained in this volume. We appreciate not only having had access to the folklore files in the institute, but also the assistance of the ISR staff in copying materials for us. We should like to express our gratitude for being given permission to publish some of the examples from the institute's files.

Introduction

Since the publication of *Urban Folklore from the Paperwork Empire*, henceforth abbreviated UF, it has become increasingly apparent to us that the invention and rapid diffusion of office copier folklore represents a major form of tradition in modern America. We have found many additional versions and variants of the approximately one hundred examples in that volume, data that provide even more evidence, though none was needed, of the traditionality of these materials. We indicated that we were limiting ourselves to a representative sampling of some of the genres of urban office folklore. However, some readers of UF have assumed that we presented an all-inclusive, exhaustive collection. In fact, we barely scratched the surface—as any reader of the present volume will easily see.

Even in this second volume, we do not claim to have reported every single item circulating in the office copier tradition. For one thing, some of the items are close to pornography or are otherwise offensive (e.g., racist). We were amused by the response of some of the many publishers who turned down our first volume for publication; they thought that the materials contained in it were beyond the bounds of good taste. Those examples were mild compared with the items we chose not to present. In this second volume, we have included some items that some readers may find distasteful, but we believe that all the data presented are essential for a documentation of the full range of the tradition. Nevertheless, we have omitted some traditional items that in our judgment would offend many readers and prevent the publishing of the book. For the materials that are in this volume, we make no apology. We do not believe we should be held responsible for the sexual content of much of the material (e.g., the cartoons). We are merely reporting an active part of American folklore. We might observe that the items selected for inclusion were taken from a corpus of nearly five hundred distinct copier folklore traditions circulating in the United States.

In this book, we have given not only additional examples of some of the categories discussed in our first volume, but have included other categories such as business cards, greeting cards, mottoes, and parodies. In our discussion of these categories, we again make no claim of having been exhaustive. We have not attempted to present every version of every item in our collection, because for some we have several dozen versions.

The eight divisions of the volume do not represent hard-and-fast categories. They group such materials as (1) definitions and wordplay, (2) business cards, (3) greeting cards and letters, (4) notices, mottoes, and awards, (5) instructions and tests, (6) cartoons and drawings, (7) double entendres, and (8) parodies. The classificatory problem is typified by, for example, parody being present throughout the volume in all the categories. Sometimes a cartoon appears in miniature on a greeting card or business card. Similarly, the device of double entendre is found in examples of wordplay and greeting cards. Many items could easily fit into several of the categories. On the other hand, some of the folk poems and jokes that circulate in copier tradition do not fit comfortably into any of the categories. Our policy was that items being transmitted ought to be included somehow even if we had to interpret our classificatory boundaries a bit loosely. Better that, we thought, than to be bound by our analytic categories. Our point is that it is the materials that are of importance. Our classificatory categories are simply necessary evils employed to provide some semblance of logical order.

Our criteria for inclusion of items are multiple existence, variation, and transmission by way of the office copier. We are not concerned with questions of origins. It is possible or likely that there are individual creators for every item. Our point is that an item, however or whenever created, becomes authentic folklore once it has undergone repetition and variation. We have multiple versions—with variation—of almost all the items. A few versions are attributed to named persons, but we have found that the attributions vary, suggesting that one or more persons may have claimed to be the author of an item. Where we have such attributions we have included them; we have no desire to present materials without giving credit to a known author. However, al-

When You're up to Your Ass in Alligators . . .

most all do not indicate an author. We make no proprietary claim on the individual items we present. As folklorists, we are preserving some examples from urban folk.

In general, we have not included items (e.g., jokes) that, though occasionally transmitted by means of the office copier, continue to flourish in oral tradition. To be sure, we have included several of those that appear to be especially popular in copier-transmitted repertoires. It is moot how much of an effect the office copier will have on the content of oral tradition. Probably both oral and office copier tradition will coexist with some reciprocal influence. For example, parodies of "The Night before Christmas" certainly existed in oral tradition long before the invention of the office copier. It seems to us that only a few talented raconteurs performed these lengthy pseudoepic poems. The office copier has greatly aided the transmission and diffusion of these classic pieces of folklore; now anyone with access to a copier can "perform" such items. In sum, items commonly transmitted by office copier have been included even though they may also be found in oral tradition. Our position is not that we wish to exclude oral materials but that we wish to include hitherto neglected written folklore materials passed on by the copy machine. We did not treat bumper stickers, graffiti, or the comments written on buttons because these materials, although worthy of study, are not in the corpus of office copier-transmitted materials.

We have presented complete, unexpurgated texts. We should not have to defend this. On the contrary, to present edited and censored texts would not only be dishonest, but would preclude the texts from being of value as American sociological documents. We have indicated whenever possible when and where an item was collected. Some of the older materials lack this minimal information and that is why it is occasionally absent in this volume. We have made every effort to use the folk titles of the items. Where there were alternate titles, we tried to select the one that was the most common in our sample. Where all the versions of an item in our corpus were untitled, we tried to create a suitable title by taking a sentence or phrase from the text of the item. Because we have included the titles of items as part of the texts, readers can see that in most instances, the title of the item corresponds exactly to the title of at least one version of the item included.

We have tried to locate parallel texts, but because academics, with one or two exceptions, have refused serious consideration of these materials until now, it has been extremely difficult to find many parallels in print even where we are certain of a given item's popularity for several decades. Some parallels with insightful commentaries we found in Gershon Legman's two-volume magnum opus devoted to erotic humor, *Rationale of the Dirty Joke* (1968) and *No Laughing Matter* (1975). However, Legman sometimes only alludes to a tradition without citing a full text. In other instances, for his purposes of analysis, he is content simply to give a short synopsis of an item rather than a complete transcript. The synopsis was sufficient for us to determine that it represented a parallel to one of our texts, but even the best synopsis is no substitute for a full text. Equally valuable for comparative annotative purposes were the two excellent collections of copier materials from Colorado by Michael Preston and his associates. The two volumes *Urban Folklore from Colorado: Typescript Broadsides* (1976) and *Urban Folklore from Colorado: Photocopy Cartoons* (1976) are a major contribution to the documentation of the traditions examined in this volume. Our only criticism is that these volumes present only raw data with little or no analysis. If Legman erred in shortchanging his texts in favor of analytic commentary, Preston and his colleagues went to the other extreme. Also, because these volumes are published only on demand (by University Microfilms), they may not be as widely distributed as they deserve to be. The same lack of analysis applies to two English collections, Nicolas Locke's *You Want It When?!! The Complete Office Graffiti* (1979) and *Office Graffiti 2* (1981) but not to an excellent sampling of German examples, Uli Kutter's *Ich Kundige!!!* (1982) where there is considerable analytic commentary.

We should like to explain our position about analysis. We obviously favor it. But the reader should realize that every item in this collection is a separate research problem. In theory, an article or sometimes an entire monograph could be devoted to a single item. It would be premature to make detailed analyses now. Our inclusion of many items represents the first time that they have appeared in print in a scholarly communication. No one could have expected the Grimm brothers to have written monographs on each of the tales published in their *Kinder und Hausmärchen*. One hundred years elapsed before the great scholarly comparative notes to the Grimm tales appeared: J. Bolte and Georg Polivka's *Anmerkungen zu den Kinder und Hausmärchen der Brüder Grimm* (1913–18). And, to this day, many of the less popular Grimm tales have yet to be studied in depth. (One can see this at a glance by browsing through Antti Aarne and Stith Thompson, *The Types of the Folktale* [second revision, 1961] and noting all the tale types that do not have double asterisks in the bibliographical references after each plot synopsis. Double asterisks indicate that a detailed if not definitive essay or monograph has been devoted to the tale. Even a cursory inspection will reveal that almost all Indo-European folktales have not yet been the subject of study.)

We bother to make this point because of the difficulties we encountered in publishing UF, which was our first attempt to investigate this area of folkloristics. For some reason it is perfectly all right to publish anthologies of favorite folktales told around the world or long lists of place names, proverbs, superstitions, and the like with no analysis whatsoever. Dozens of monographs in folklore publications series reflect this "texts only" bias. But critics of UF and no doubt of this volume will ask why we did not write a complete integrated analysis of American society using our texts as points of departure. This would be a laudable goal, but it is not ours, at least not now. We do not pretend to be sociologists or experts in American studies. We are folklorists who have collected an unusual array of folkloristic materials previously not available to members of any discipline. We believe these materials reflect major concerns in American values and worldview and that they represent an almost unexplored area in symbolic communication and humor. We have attempted to suggest some of these topics and themes, especially those reiterated throughout our corpus: the emphasis on sexuality, the battle of the sexes, the unending struggle against bureaucracy, the concern with ethnicity, the anxieties produced by the demands of the success ethic, and the escape into parody.

Many readers will recognize some of the items as ones they have seen somewhere before. Because these items are folklore, that is to be expected. All are traditional and will therefore be familiar to some readers. However, it is extremely doubtful that any one reader will have seen all the items. Moreover, if one had been interested in doing so, it is difficult to imagine how that might have been accomplished. The corpus of materials has only recently been the subject of any serious inquiry. Except our previous book, the above-mentioned useful office copier collections from Colorado, and the representative sampling of English and German materials, there are no extensive published collections of these materials. One could look in vain in standard collections of folklore or humor for examples of office copier traditions. Yet they are extremely widespread and popular. Many have been in circulation for decades. But the lack of attention paid them by folklorists and students of American culture has made it difficult for us to document the age and extent of many of them.

The data we are presenting should interest any student of twentieth-century American society. Sociologists, historians, psychologists, linguists, and others should find these materials of value. No one concerned with American humor or American national character should ignore the unique self-portrait of a people drawn from the urban folklore of the paperwork empire.

Abbreviations

Because there has been little scholarly attention paid to the materials presented in this volume, there is no point in including a bibliography of sources consulted. The few previous relevant studies, Gershon Legman's two encyclopedic discussions of erotic humor, *Rationale of the Dirty Joke* and *No Laughing Matter* and the two volumes of office copier folklore from Colorado, proved to be highly useful for annotation. Because we cite these sources often, we have used the following abbreviations:

IK	Uli Kutter, *Ich Kundige!!! Zeugnisse von Wünschen und Ängsten am Arbeitsplatz—Eine Bestandsaufnahme* (Marburg: Jonas Verlag, 1982)
ISR	Institute for Sex Research, 416 Morrison Hall, Indiana University, Bloomington, Indiana 47401
NLM	G. Legman, *No Laughing Matter: Rationale of the Dirty Joke—An Analysis of Sexual Humor, Second Series* (New York: Breaking Point, 1975)
OG2	Nicolas Locke, *Office Graffiti 2* (London: Proteus Books, 1981)
RDJ	G. Legman, *Rationale of the Dirty Joke—An Analysis of Sexual Humor, First Series* (New York: Grove Press, 1968)
TCB	Paul Smith, *The Complete Book of Office Mis-Practice* (London: Routledge & Kegan Paul, 1984)
UF	Alan Dundes and Carl R. Pagter, *Urban Folklore from the Paperwork Empire* (Austin: American Folklore Society, 1975)
UFFC-PC	Louis Michael Bell, Cathy Makin Orr, and Michael James Preston, *Urban Folklore from Colorado: Photocopy Cartoons* (Ann Arbor: Xerox University Microfilms, 1976)

UFFC-TB   Cathy Makin Orr and Michael James Preston, *Urban Folklore from Colorado: Typescript Broadsides* (Ann Arbor: Xerox University Microfilms, 1976)

YD   Wayne B. Norris, *You Don't Have to be Crazy to Work Here ... But It Sure Helps* (Los Angeles: Price/Stern/Sloan, 1986)

YWIW   Nicolas Locke, *You Want It When?!! The Complete Office Graffiti* (London: Proteus Books, 1979)

Coming to Terms

Wordplay is actively represented in the folklore transmitted by office copier. The range of materials extends from pseudo-dictionary definitions and in-group argot to long lists of punning one-liners. Many of the definitions or one-liners surely antedate the advent of the office copier. Yet what was once laboriously copied by hand or run off by ditto machine or mimeograph can now be reproduced and passed on with ease thanks to the Xerox machine or its equivalent.

The marked improvement in communications technology has resulted in the increased exposure of until now esoteric jargons to public view. This has led to the realization that what a given group says may not be what that group necessarily means. One reason for the discrepancy may be the influence of commercial advertising in which exaggerated claims and superlatives are commonplace. On the other hand, many individuals are not fooled by the rhetorical overkill. Still, part of the initiation rite in joining any urban group is mastering the intricacies and subtleties of a set of key terms. Surely one of the most interesting types of office copier folklore presented in this category are tongue-in-cheek translations from jargon into understandable English.

1. The Modern Dictionary (Webster Unexpurgated)

The following item was collected in Seattle, Washington, in 1953, and is deposited in the Folklore File in the library of the Institute for Sex Research (ISR) at Indiana University. It contains more than eighty definitions and is therefore one of the most extensive versions of this kind of material.

Adolescence — An intermediate stage between purity and adultery.

Adultery — The wrong people doing the right thing.

Alimony — The screwing you get for the screwing you got.

Amnesiac — A man who can't remember where he laid his last wife.

Angel — A female spirit who probably spends most of her time wishing she could trade her harp for an upright organ.

Aviatricks — A pilot who cannot fly upside down without a crack-up nor right side up without having a bust up.

Baby — A hollow tube with a loud voice at one end and a complete lack of responsibility at the other.

Bachelor — A man who has no children to speak of; one who has done without marriage.

Bachelor Girl — One who has never been married. (See Old Maid)

Balls — The chief requisite accessory for such games as basketball and football. No sporting man is without one or two.

Barefoot Party — Where you take off your shoes and hose.

Bathroom Menace — A man having the misfortune at a tender age to have been circumcised by a cross-eyed rabbi.

Blackout — The reason a girl is apt to be blown into maternity without knowing who is responsible.

Boudoir — No man's land.

Brassiere — An awning over a child's restaurant; mezzanine jockstrap; titty hammock; a device which makes mountains out of molehills, and vice versa; double-barreled slingshot.

Cannibal — One who is apt to pass his best friend.

Castrated Dinosaur	A colossal fossil with a docile tassel.
Chivalry	A man's inclination to defend a woman against every man but himself.
Complications	A confused situation that makes it difficult to get at the works; for instance, a knock-kneed virgin.
Conscience	That which hurts when everything else feels so good.
Constipation	To have and to hold.
Cookie	A virgin doughnut.
Dachshund	A low-down son of a bitch.
Dance	A naval engagement without the loss of seamen.
Dead Stick	When the spirit is willing but the flesh is weak.
Decoy	A flashlight in the pants pocket.
Deferred	What a Spar, Wave, or Wac gets by jumping over a bonfire.
Diary	Book of Revelations.
Divorce	What happens when two people cannot stomach each other any longer.
Doctor	A lucky fellow who is privileged to undress women and go all over them without getting his face slapped.
Drake, Sir Francis	The man who circumcised the world with a forty-foot cutter.
Enema	A goose with a gush.
Exploration	Beating around the bush.
Father's Day	Nine months before Labor Day.
Furlough	What a Spar, Wave, or Wac gets by squatting.
Gentleman	One who is always careful, after goosing a young lady, to restore her dress to its former position; one who is always careful to rest at least half his weight on his elbows.
Gigilo	The egg that laid the golden goose.
Giraffe Party	All neck and no tail.
Glamour Girl	A much-publicized young lady who is full of oomph, and frequently full of other things; one who doesn't worry about the meat shortage.
Horse Show	A lot of horses showing their asses to a lot of horses' asses showing their horses.
Husband	What is left of a lover after the nerve has been killed.

Coming to Terms

Kept Woman	One who wears mink all day and fox all night.
Hung Chow	Chinese constipation.
Kiss	Upstairs shopping for downstairs merchandise; upper persuasion for lower invasion.
Lousy Bastard	One who sits and scratches himself while his father and mother are being married.
Marriage	A lottery in which the prize winner draws alimony.
Masturbation	A solo played on a private organ.
Maternity Dress	A zoot suit with a rape shape.
Metallurgist	A man who can look at a platinum blonde and tell whether she is virgin metal or common ore.
Minute Man	One who double-parks while he visits a sporting house.
Mistress	Something between a mister and a mattress.
Morning	The time of day when the rising generation retires, and the retiring generation arises.
Mother's Day	Nine months after Father's Day.
Mule Barbecue	Where everybody gets a piece of ass.
Nun	A woman who ain't never had none, don't want none, and ain't going to get none.
Nursery	A place to park last year's fun until it grows up a bit.
Old Maid	A woman of uncertain age who ain't never been married nor nothing. A "Yes" girl who has never had a chance to talk.
Outdoor Girl	One with the bloom of youth on her cheeks and the cheeks of youth in her bloomers.
Pansy	A man who likes his vice versa.
Pajamas	Items of clothing that newlyweds place beside the bed for use in case of fire.
Papoose	Consolation prize for taking a chance on an Indian blanket.
Passion	The feeling you feel when you feel you are going to feel a feeling you have never felt before.
Pimp	A crack salesman, a nookie bookie.
Pregnancy	When a woman is all swelled up over her mate's handiwork.
Private Secretary	A stenographer who watches her periods.

When You're up to Your Ass in Alligators . . .

Psychiatrist	One who tries to find out whether an infant has more fun in infancy than an adult does in adultery.
Puppy Love	The beginning of a dog's life.
Quack	A pwace to put a pwick.
Rape	Seduction without salesmanship; assault with intent to please.
Rumba	An asset to music.
Sin	Anything the other fellow enjoys and you don't.
Sissy	A man that gets out of the bathtub to take a leak.
Sob Sister	A girl who sits on your lap and bawls and makes it hard for you.
Spring Fever	When the iron in your blood turns to lead in your pants.
Stepins	A lady's last line of defense; they go on easily but must be coaxed off.
Stork	The bird that has none of the fun of bringing babies.
Sympathetic Secretary	A girl who sits on the boss's lap and bawls while his business goes in the hole.
Taxidermist	A man who mounts animals; a sheepherder.
Tomcat	A ball-bearing mouse trap.
Triplets	Taking seriously what was poked at you in fun.
Uncanny	A house without a toilet.
Union Suit	What a woman wears to avoid labor trouble.
Vice	Anything you enjoy that is bad for you.
Virginity	A bubble on the stream of life—one prick and it is gone forever.
Virgin Wool	That from a sheep which can run faster than the shepherd.

We should note that we have left the original spelling as we found it. Folklorists who work with written or printed texts know very well that spelling peculiarities and "mistakes" often provide valuable clues to determining the relationship of one text to another. (If both texts contain the same misspelling or same order of details, they may well be cognate.) For this reason, we did not change "gigilo" to "gigolo" (and we refrained from placing *sic* in brackets). Other lists of definitions that have "gigilo" or have "pajamas" following "pansy" out of alphabetical order may thus be compared with the one we have presented here.

Many of the above definitions have been traditional for decades. For example, in *Anecdota Americana* (New York: Nesor Publishing Company, 1934), pp. 38 and 108, we find "Marriage is a lottery in which the prize winner draws alimony" and "Rape: Assault with intent to please." Some of the definitions are dated. For example, the zoot suit (in the Maternity Dress definition) was popular in the late 1930s and early 1940s. Readers unfamiliar with the suit will not recognize the play on its "drape shape."

No two versions of the list are exactly the same—which is what one would expect in dealing with folklore. From other versions we give some of the definitions not included in the list above:

Clergyman   A man who works to beat hell.
Courtship   Extended period of shopping, mostly of the window variety.
Discretion   Ability not to do those things in youth which constitute the vain regrets of old age.
Fornication   What bad people do and get caught at, and what good people do and don't get caught at.
Nurse   A panhandler.
Prostitutes   Busy bodies.
Spouse   A combined domestic servant, hot water bottle and incubator.
Spring   When a young man's fancy turns to what a young woman has been thinking about all winter.
Stockings   Feminine pedal covering that generally neither comes up to milady's expectations nor tickles her fancy.
Twins   Womb mates that eventually become bosom friends.
Underdog   A bitch.
Virgin   An ugly third-grader.
Wife   A gadget that you screw on the bed and it does your housework for you.

In a version from San Francisco in 1971, entitled "Daffynitions," containing thirty entries, one finds such examples as:

Blotter   Something you look for while the ink dries.
Boy   A noise with dirt on it.

Hell	What you get in the morning for raising at night.
Nothing	A balloon with the skin peeled off.
Professor	One who talks in someone else's sleep.
Sleep	That which when you are coming in at 2:00 A.M., Pa ain't a.

There are blatant sexism and male chauvinism in some of the definitions. One must remember, however, that folklore reflects a society's values. One should not blame the mirror for an ugly image. On the other hand, to the extent that folklore molds values rather than mirrors them, one must be concerned in presenting texts that contain stereotypes of racism, sexism, and ethnic or religious groups. Our position is that the folklore exists whether it is studied by folklorists or not. If one is anxious to attack particular stereotypes, one must have the evidence of the nature of the stereotypes in hand. There is always a risk in presenting ethnic slurs and comparable folkloristic data that the audience will remember only the slurs and not the point that thinking in stereotypes is not only unfair but dangerous. Because the folklore circulates, we feel that the presentation of folklore containing items that may be offensive to some readers is a risk worth taking. Censoring or repressing the folklore would not solve the problem in society that led to the creation and diffusion of the folklore in the first place.

For other definitions in print like the above, see Harold H. Hart, *The Complete Immortalia* (New York: Bell Publishing Company, 1971), pp. 126–27 and Alan Dundes and Robert A. Georges, "Some Minor Genres of Obscene Folklore," *Journal of American Folklore* 75 (1962): 223–24.

There are related forms involving several rhyming definitions ending with a pseudoquestion. Consider the following text collected in Kokomo, Indiana, in 1976:

If a bra is a upper topper flopper stopper,
A jock strap is a lower decker pecker checker,
And gold toilet paper is a super duper pooper scooper,
What is a punch drunk Japanese boxer, whose father has diarrhea?

Answer: A slap happy Jappy with a crap happy pappy.

2. Psychedelirium Tremens

Conventional dictionaries inevitably lag far behind current usage. The folk have tried to close the gap by compiling lexicons of new words or old words with new meanings. In Psychedelirium Tremens, there is more than a hint of discontent with the fast-changing pace of modern language. Old words have been expropriated and endowed with new life and meaning. These new meanings are so well established that they need not be given. It is rather the citation of the older meanings that provides the basis for the humor. (Any reader in doubt as to the modern meanings of the emphasized words may consult Wentworth and Flexner, *Dictionary of American Slang* (New York, 1967.) For another version of the text, see UFFC-TB, 127. For a version from England, see TCB, 172.) The text below was collected in San Francisco in 1968.

PSYCHEDELIRIUM TREMENS

Remember when HIPPIE meant big in the hips and a TRIP involved travel in cars, planes and ships?

When POT was a vessel for cooking things in, and HOOKED was what Grandmother's rug might have been?

When FIX was a verb that meant mend or repair, and BE-IN meant existing somewhere?

When NEAT meant well organized, tidy and clean, and GRASS was a ground-cover, normally green?

When lights and not people were SWITCHED ON AND OFF, and the PILL might have been what you took for a cough?

When CAMP meant to quarter outdoors in a tent, and POP was what the weasel went?

When GROOVY meant furrowed with channels and hollows, and BIRDS were winged creatures, like robins and swallows?

When FUZZ was a substance that's fluffy like lint, and BREAD came from bakeries, not from the mint?

When SQUARE meant a 90-degree angled form, and COOL was
a temperature not quite warm?

When ROLL meant a bun, and ROCK was a stone, and HANG-
UP was something you did to a phone?

When CHICKEN meant poultry, and BAG meant a sack, and
JUNK trashy cast-offs and old bric-a-brac?

When JAM was preserves that you spread on your bread, and
CRAZY meant balmy, not right in the head?

When CAT was a feline, a kitten grown up, and TEA was a liquid
you drank from a cup?

When SWINGER was someone who swung in a swing, and PAD
was a soft sort of cushiony thing?

When WAY OUT meant distant and far, far away, and a man
couldn't sue you for calling him GAY?

When DIG meant to shovel and spade in the dirt, and PUT-ON
was what you would do with a skirt?

When TOUGH described meat too unyielding to chew, and MAK-
ING A SCENE was a rude thing to do?

Words once so sensible, sober and serious are making the FREAK
SCENE like PSYCHEDELIRIOUS.

It's GROOVY, MAN, GROOVY, but English it's not,
Methinks that the language has gone straight to POT.

3. What People Say

Anyone who has ever spoken a foreign language in a foreign
country has undoubtedly learned that there is a great difference
between what people say and what people really mean. The distinction is equally valid in one's own native language. However,

usually, one has learned that "We really must get together one of these days" is a kind of friendly closing formula before leave-taking, which reflects no genuine intent to arrange a get-together in the immediate future. The following item collected in Indianapolis in 1976 attempts to translate some common idioms in American speech.

WHAT PEOPLE SAY	WHAT THEY MEAN
What is your expert opinion of my . . . ?	I've scratched your back and you should scratch mine.
Did you hear the joke about the . . . ?	If you did, don't say anything—just get ready to laugh.
Why, anyone can do it!	I find it simple, therefore it is simple, therefore, anyone who isn't a moron can do it.
I'm not suggesting anything.	No. I'm telling you.
What's the use . . . ?	I can't cope any longer.
Mind your own business—or stay out of this.	I'm losing the argument.
How do you like my outfit, my proposal?	Please, reassure me. Don't criticize.
You don't think something's happened, do you?	I think something has happened.
It's not the money, it's the principle.	It's the money.
I would never do that.	That frightens me, or, I secretly like it and might do it if I had the chance.
If you will grant X, Y and Z, I will . . .	Play it my way, or I won't play at all.
That's nothing, or—It may interest you . . .	I'm smarter, richer or better than you.
We're such a happy couple.	It's true; I'm happy and I feel guilty about it; or I'm afraid we're going to split up?
Frankly, I think our demands are not excessive.	I think they are, but will try to get them anyway.
Of course, I wouldn't hold you to those terms.	Yes, I would.

When You're up to Your Ass in Alligators . . .

When I was your age . . .	I'm all-wise, indoctrinating and infallible.
Boy, do I have a deal for you:	I sure do—a bad one; or, I'm not really sure about it.
I'd like to see it done this way.	I'm the only one who thinks around here.
On the whole or under the circumstances . . .	I don't have any specific strong point so I'll generalize.
Let me sleep on it.	It's not important enough to keep me awake.
In view of that fact, or, Considering that . . .	I'm, or it's, too good to refuse.
Of course, I love you but give me a little more time.	I want to shop around.
Do you think we're doing the right thing?	We're not doing the right thing.
Are you getting anything out of this?	Neither one of us are getting anything.
Would you like me a bit more if . . . ?	Please, approve of me.
I really can't stay.	I want to stay all night.
I can't go there, looking like this.	Don't make me clean up.
I'll never speak to you again.	Make me talk.
Is that clear? Okay? Check?	I doubt you are capable of understanding.
I was just going to say . . .	I wasn't going to say that at all.

This format with its undercutting definitions lends itself for use in a variety of professional contexts. The results sometimes appear in company newsletters and other ephemeral media. For example, a real estate glossary in the same vein appeared in *Frankly Speaking* (August 1974), an advertising newsletter issued by the firm of Clinton E. Frank, Inc.

COLONIAL—built prior to the second Eisenhower Administration.
GRACIOUS COLONIAL—you can't afford it.
VICTORIAN—drafty.
LEISURE HOME—habitable during July and August only.

CHALET—ranch-style but set on a steep slope; with shutters.

OLDER HOME—pre-earthquake; lists disconcertingly.

IDEAL FOR YOUNG COUPLE—if they're elves.

PATIO—in the West, an undulating backyard full of cracked brick; in the East, a spot near the back door where the cement truck overturned.

PIAZZA—porch.

GLEAMING BATHROOM—bathroom.

VANITY BATHROOM—bathroom with a table nailed to the wall.

CONVENIENT TO SHOPPING—bay window overlooks Safeway parking lot.

FAMILY ROOM—basement with 100-watt light bulb.

ATTIC PLAYROOM—crawl space under the eaves.

NEEDS SOME FIXING UP—leg of bathtub protruding through kitchen ceiling needs polishing.

BROOK ON PROPERTY—goes through the cellar in the winter; dry all summer.

DESIRABLE CORNER—corner.

ENTRANCE FOYER—door.

ONLY 20 MINUTES FROM CITY—by telephone.

FIRST OFFERING—since yesterday.

GOOD TERMS ON REMAINING CHOICE HOMES—leftover lemons.

EXCELLENT MOVE-IN CONDITION—for painters and carpenters.

SEEING IS BELIEVING—seeing is believing.

Similarly, the *PSA California Magazine* for August 1975 contained a brief set of restaurant descriptions.

Dining Out Definitions

Real Home Cooking—None of our dishes have foreign names.

We Do Not Serve Alcoholic Beverages—Our lawyer has spent $35,000 and still hasn't come up with a liquor permit.

Open Kitchen—Smoke gets in your eyes.

Organic Vegetables—Who can tell, but you gotta trust somebody.

Leisurely Dining—Our waitresses have bunions and take their own sweet time.

Rustic Setting—The parking lot has not been hard-surfaced yet.

Ask About Private Parties—Yeah, and let us know where there is one.

Genuine Dover Sole—With the overpowering sauce, you'll never know.

Exotic Cocktails—These are always a surprise provided by our bartender. He drinks.

Old World Atmosphere—During heavy rains, the roof may leak.

4. Ode to the Four-Letter Word

The folk themselves have commented at some length on the Anglo-American reluctance to refer to anatomical parts and bodily functions by their pungent earthy names, preferring instead to employ Latinate substitutes. Until the last decade or so, one rarely encountered "four-letter words" in respectable contemporary literary works. Even scholarly journals scrupulously avoided using the so-called dirty words, resorting to dashes, asterisks, or Latin translation. Perhaps the most elaborate commentary is a series of folk verses employing rhymed couplets. Legman (RDJ, 222) calls this item "unquestionably the most popular erotic folk-poem in America during World War II." The text presented here is from ISR, dated 1960, from upstate New York. Vance Randolph included a version in his valuable "Vulgar Rhymes from the Ozarks" (1954 manuscript on deposit in ISR), a version collected from Columbia, Missouri, dating from 1944. For versions in print, see *The Complete Immortalia* (New York, 1971), pp. 410–13; Harold Hart, *Poems Lewd and Lusty* (New York, 1976), pp. 135–38.

ODE TO THE FOUR LETTER WORD

Banish the use of the four letter words,
Whose meanings are never obscure;
The Angles and Saxons, those bawdy old birds,
Were vulgar, obscene, and impure.

But cherish the use of the weasling phrase
That never quite says what you mean;
You'd better be known for your hypocrite ways,
Than as vulgar, impure, and obscene.

When nature is calling plain speaking out,
When ladies, God bless them, are milling about,
You may wee-wee, make water, or empty the glass,
You may powder your nose, even "Jonnie" may pass;
Shake the dew of the lily, see a man about a dog,
When everybody's soused, it's condensing the fog.
But please do remember, if you want to know bliss,
Not only in Shakespeare do characters piss.

A woman has bosoms, a bust, or a breast,
Those lily white swellings that bulge 'neath her vest;
They are towers of ivory, or sheaves of new wheat,
In a moment of passion, ripe apples to eat.
You may speak of her nipples as fingers of fire,
With hardly a question of raising her ire;
But by Rabelais' beard, she will throw several fits,
If you speak of them rudely as good honest tits.

It's a "Cavern of Joy" you are thinking of now,
A "warm tender field awaiting a plow";
It's a quivering pigeon caressing your hand,
Or the national anthem—it makes all stand.
Or perhaps it's a flower, a grotto, a well,
The hope of the world or a velvety hell;
But, friend, heed this warning, beware the affront
Of aping the Saxon—don't call it a cunt.

Though a lady repell your advance, she'll be kind
As long as you intimate what's on your mind;
You may tell her you're hungry, you need to be swung,
You may ask her to see how your etchings are hung.
Or you may mention the ashes that need to be hauled,
Put the lid on her saucepan, even lay's not too bold;
But the moment you're forthright get ready to duck,
For the girl isn't born yet who'll stand for "let's fuck."

When You're up to Your Ass in Alligators . . .

So banish the words that Elizabeth used
When she was a queen on the throne,
The modern maid's virtue is easily bruised
By the four letter words all alone.
Let your morals be loose as an alderman's vest,
If your language is always obscure;
Today not the act, but the word is the test
Of the vulgar, obscene, and impure.

5. I Think I'm Stagnant

The two codes, that is, the genteel and the vulgar, sometimes seriously impede the communication process. Nowhere is the discrepancy between the codes more crucial than in the hospital setting where embarrassed patients may be unable to speak freely about their ailments. In some instances, doctors and nurses may be equally embarrassed by the direct use of the vernacular terms. It is of interest that a compilation entitled *A Manual of English for the Overseas Doctor* by Joy E. Parkinson (Edinburgh: E & S Livingstone, 1969) specifically includes a section entitled "Colloquial English" so as to inform doctors about slang terms they are likely to encounter. According to Parkinson, the patient is sometimes so inarticulate that the doctor is forced to use the popular idioms to determine precisely what the patient's problems are. The following text collected from Kokomo, Indiana, in 1976, plays on the nurse's concern for proper terminology as opposed to concern for the patient's condition. (For a version told about a "Southern gal at hospital information desk," see J. M. Elgart, *More over Sexteen* [New York: Grayson, 1953], p. 60.)

A girl walked up to the information desk at a Hospital and asked to see the "uptern."

"I think you mean the 'intern,' don't you?" asked the nurse on duty.

"Yes, I guess I do," said the girl. "I want to have a 'contamination.'"

"You mean 'examination,'" corrected the nurse.

"Well, I want to go to the fraternity ward, anyway."

"I'm sure," said the nurse, "that you're thinking of the 'maternity' ward."

To which the girl replied loudly, "Uptern, intern; contamination, examination; fraternity, maternity . . . what's the difference? All I know is I haven't demonstrated in two months and I think I'm stagnant!"

6. Timbuktu

The conversion of innocent speech into sexually suggestive statements can be accomplished through clever wordplay. The following poetic verbal duel between Lord Byron and Shakespeare contrasts once again the genteel with the vulgar. The folk are quite right, actually, to credit Shakespeare with such skills. See the entries for "come" and "poperin pear" among others in Eric Partridge, *Shakespeare's Bawdy* (New York: E. P. Dutton, 1960). The first version presented here was collected in Oakland in 1976; the second was collected in Fremont in 1979.

Shakespeare and Lord Byron died and went to heaven together. Saint Peter, who met them at the pearly gates, was very embarrassed. It seemed he only had accommodations for one person. So, in order to be fair, he told the men he was going to test them. They were each to write some poetry, with one stipulation: the poetry must contain the word *Timbuktu*. So, Shakespeare and Lord Byron each found a tree and sat down to write poetry. Byron finished first, found Saint Peter, and read him his poetry:

> As I stand upon the dry and burning sands
> And gaze beyond the vast wastelands,
> There suddenly appears in view
> A caravan from Timbuktu.

Saint Peter told Lord Byron this was very good. Shakespeare then declared his poetry was ready to be read, and his went like this:

> Tim and I a-hunting went.
> We came upon three maidens in a tent.

Since they were three
And we but two,
I bucked one
And Tim bucked two!

Poets Keats and Homer died and Saint Peter said there was only room for one in heaven. To determine which one, Saint Peter asked them to write a poem in sixty seconds using the word *Timbucktoo.*

Keats wrote:

As I was walking on the shore
listening to the ocean roar
A sailing ship came into view
Destination TIMBUCKTOO.

Homer wrote:

As Tim and I astrolling went,
We spied 3 maidens in a tent.
Since they were 3 and we were 2
I bucked one and Tim bucked two.

7. The New Bus Driver

Another type of urban folklore that deals with the playful use of language concerns the inability of a character to articulate a word or phrase. In this sense, the items are analogous to tongue twisters or spooneristic conundrums. (For examples of spooneristic conundrums, see Alan Dundes and Robert A. Georges, "Some Minor Genres of Obscene Folklore," *Journal of American Folklore* 75 [1962]: 222.) In theory, these linguistic routines could be entirely in oral tradition, but in practice they are often encountered in the copier format. Because these materials commonly depend for their impact on the taboos against uttering obscenities in public, they illustrate the continuing apprehension of American children and adults about exposure to "dirty words."

The following text relates a bus driver's misadventure. The version presented here was collected in 1965 but was in circulation at Hamilton High School in West Los Angeles in the late 1950s. It was carried around by high school boys in their wallets and would be read aloud to male peers. (For a variant, see Legman, NLM, 809.)

The Hotel Astor hired a new bus driver and instructed him to meet all the trains at the Pennsylvania Station, and to announce in a loud voice, "Free bus to the Hotel Astor." Enroute to the station he kept repeating to himself, "Free bus to the Hotel Astor." But upon arrival of the first train he became confused and suddenly started yelling: "Free ass at the Hotel Buster I mean—Free hotel at the bust your Astor I mean—Bust your ass at the hotel freezer I mean—Freeze your ass at the hotel bastard—free hotel ass buster—I mean I mean kiss my ass you bastards, and take a streetcar—I quit."

8. Port or Sherry

The comparison of proper and improper language often suggests that the brevity and directness of colloquial speech is infinitely superior to the sesquipedalian prose required by the norms of etiquette. The first text from ISR was collected during World War II. The second text, about a choice between beer and champagne, was collected in Irvine, California, in 1976. Legman cites several texts (RDJ, 340) including one from New York City dated 1938 (NLM, 874).

It seems a wealthy playboy out for the night flirted with a lovely young girl at the bar and at length, escorted her to his apartment. Instead of being a tramp, she was well groomed, chic, and apparently most intellectual. Thinking he must impress her to get anywhere, he exhibited a few etchings, old prints, and first editions and finally produced some wine. He asked if she would prefer Port or Sherry.

"Oh, Sherry by all means," she answered. "Sherry to me is just nectar of the Gods. Just gazing at it in the crystal clear decanter fills me with anticipation of a strange and heavenly thrill, and as the stopper is lifted out, the gorgeous liquid slides, serpent-like, into the goblet, I inhale the exotic and tangy fumes, and am carried off on the soft wings of ecstasy. Furthermore, when actually sipping this tantalizing potion, my entire being simply glows, and while a thousand velvety violins throb in my ears, I am tenderly lifted into a new and more exquisitely beautiful world."

"On the other hand," she said, "Port makes me fart."

BEER OR CHAMPAGNE

A distinguished-appearing gentleman having been introduced to a demure young lady, invited her into the cocktail lounge for a drink. Inquiring as to whether she preferred beer or champagne, she replied: "Oh, I would prefer champagne. When I drink champagne my head gets all bubbly and I have the loveliest thoughts and daydreams. I dream I am lying nude in the soft sands of a lover-like island. As I recline there in blissful content, I see a tall, handsome man approach from the beach. He comes and kneels by my side. He gazes deep into my eyes and his hands caress my body. Later, much later, he walks into the sea only to reappear with huge shells filled with beautiful pearls. These he pours over my quivering body, creating a sensation divine. When I drink beer, I fart."

9. The Lament of Juan

In this tradition, the mispronunciation is attributed to a recent immigrant's problems in speaking English. In this version dated June 1944, from San Francisco, a Mexican named Juan Ortega is the protagonist. In a version dated 1964 (not presented here), the Mexican's name is Dor Orega. Other versions (1947, 1970) cast an Italian as the main character and the locus is Chicago or Dallas.

A Mexican, Juan Ortega, on his arrival in Fort Worth from Dallas, told the following story:

You know I don lak that Dallas woth a sheet. They don got no hospitality. These morn, I go to the coffee shop for breakfast. I tol the girl, please I wan two peese toast, what you think She bring me one peese. I say lady, I wan two peese, she say if you wan two peese, go to the toilet. I say you don understand, I wan two peese on my plate. She say don you peese on your plate, you son of B. I never see that lady before in all my life, I won eat where they call me son of B, so I walk out.

I go to the Adolphus for my deener, and the lady bring me the spoon, knife and napkin, but don bring me foork. I say lady I wanna foork. She say what you talk, everybody wanna foork. I say you don understand, I wanna foork on table, she say you don care where you foork you son of B. So I figure I don eat, I go to my room.

When I get to my room, I no goota sheet on my bed, so I phone manager that I wanna sheet on bed. He say don you sheet on bed, big boy, you son of B. So when he call me son of B, I decide to check out.

I go down to check out and pay my bill, and tell that Dallas man I gonna check out and go to Fort Worth. He say, well, my friend, goodbye and peace on you. I say peese on you, you son of B because I am so mad in my face I feel lak I can whip any man twice my heavy and two times my old!

10. "You-all" Is Plural

In the United States, regionalisms in speech can be as fascinating as immigrant dialects. Among American regions, southern folk speech is especially noteworthy for its rich variety. One of the phrases that has intrigued Americans from other parts of the country is "you-all," or its contraction "y'all." It epitomizes the essence of southern speech—at least in the northern stereotype of that speech pattern.

The phrase serves a useful linguistic function. It provides a plural form of *you* in contrast to a singular form, a distinction found in many European languages, for example, *tu/vous* in French. (In western Pennsylvania, the equivalent of you-all is "you-uns" and there may well be analogous formations in other areas.) The undeniable utility of you-all is explained in a charming piece of verse collected in Bloomington, Indiana, in 1961 but reported to have circulated in North Carolina in 1940.

> Come all of you from other parts,
> Both city folks and rural,
> And listen while I tell you this.
> The word "you-all" is plural.

> When we say "you-all" come down,
> Or "we-all" shall be lonely,
> We mean a dozen folks, perhaps
> And not one person only.

> If I should say to Hiram Jones,
> For instance, "you-all's lazy",
> Or, "Will you-all lend me your knife?"
> He'd think that I was crazy.

> Now if you'd be more sociable
> And with us often mingle,
> You'd find that in the native tongue
> "You-all" is never single.

11. The Government Employee

One way of making fun of terms is by pretending they are proper names. The following joke illustrates how the names of dogs can be used to provide a definition of a term. It was collected in Oakland, California, in 1977.

THE GOVERNMENT EMPLOYEE

Three men, an Architect, a Mathematician and a Government worker, got together to brag about their dogs. Each one thought his dog was the smartest and had fantastic abilities. So they decided to show each other what their respective dogs could do.

The Architect called to his dog, T-Square, gave him a piece of chalk, and told him to draw a square, a circle and a triangle, which he did very accurately.

The Mathematician agreed that T-Square was a very remarkable dog . . . , "but let me show you what my dog can do." He called his dog, Slide Rule, and said, "I'll show you what a really smart dog can do." He told Slide Rule to go to a pile of cookies and bring back a dozen, which Slide Rule did without any hesitation. . . . "Now, Slide Rule, separate them into equal parts," and Slide Rule divided the cookies into four stacks of three each.

They agreed that was quite a feat.

Then the Government worker said he had watched both their dogs do fantastic things, "but now let me show you a really clever animal." He called his dog to him and said, "Now, Coffee Break, show them what you can do." Without hesitation, Coffee Break immediately ate all the cookies, screwed the other two dogs, and went home on sick leave.

In another version collected from a Ford Motor Company office in Detroit in 1977, the dog-owners are automobile workers from Chrysler, General Motors, and Ford. The version is like the text above except for a slight addition in the punch line: "Without hesitation, 'Coffee Break' immediately ate all the cookies, screwed the other two dogs, claimed a back injury, and went home on sick leave!!!"

The joke is also common in oral tradition. In a version known by one of the authors (an attorney), the dog-owners are a mathematician, a doctor, and a lawyer, whose dogs are named Pythagoras, Hippocrates, and Shyster. In this version, the owners are sitting around a camp fire on a hunting trip with their dogs. After a chicken dinner, they boast about the skills of their dogs. Each dog in turn demonstrates his prowess. Pythagoras arranges the chicken bones to spell out the Pythagorean theorem: $c^2 = a^2 + b^2$. Hippocrates arranges the bones into a skeletal depiction of a chicken. Shyster eats the bones and screws the other two dogs.

12. Famous Quotations Dept.

One theory of humor involves incongruity. In the present text, a well-known phrase or sentence, perhaps from a celebrated poet, perhaps from an advertising jingle, is attributed to a prominent individual, living or dead. Many of the allusions are to topical events and personalities. For example, a repeatedly shown television commercial for coffee in the 1970s pictured a man called Juan Valdez who was said to live in Colombia. He was invariably pictured picking out the best coffee beans for the company whose product was being advertised. To Mr. Valdez is attributed T. S. Eliot's line from "The Love Song of J. Alfred Prufrock": "I have measured out my life with coffee spoons." No doubt in time, some of the allusions and wit will be lost. One would need to know that Willie Sutton was a famous robber who presumably needed a "fence" to dispose of the stolen merchandise; that Hugh Downs was a television personality who acted as host of the "Today" show; that actor Tony Curtis was reported to have been accused of carrying "grass" (marijuana), and so forth. On the other hand, references to Robinson Crusoe and Oscar Wilde and some others may be understood by many future generations. This text comes from the Music Division of the Library of Congress and is dated 1970.

FAMOUS QUOTATIONS DEPT.

"Good fences make good neighbors."   Willie Sutton

"Pigeons on the grass, alas."   Tony Curtis

"A stitch in time . . ." and "The way to a man's heart is through his stomach."   Christaan Barnard

"When you're number 2 you try harder."   Spiro T. Agnew

"I got rhythm."   Pope Paul

"I never met a man I didn't like."   Oscar Wilde

"A bird in hand . . ."   L.B.J.

"Let them eat cake."   Sara Lee

"Honor thy father and thy mother."   Lizzie Borden

"I have measured out my life with coffee spoons."   Juan Váldez

"You always hurt the one you love."   Marquis de Sade

"Neither a borrower nor a lender be."   David Rockefeller

"My cup runneth over."   Raquel Welch

"Speak for yourself, John."   Martha Mitchell

First Prize:
"The sweetest sounds I ever heard are still inside my head."
   Ludwig van Beethoven

Runners-up:
"Let's run it up the flag pole and see who salutes it."   Betsy
   Ross

"Don't start something you can't finish."   Franz Schubert

"He maketh me to lie down in green pastures."   Lady Con-
   stance Chatterley

"It's a nice place to visit, but I wouldn't want to live there."
   Dante Alighieri

"Supercalifragilisticexpialidocious."   Marshall McLuhan

"Plymouth makes it!"   John Alden

"What this country needs is a good five-cent cigar."   George
   Sand

"Dr. Livingstone, I presume?"   Lewis and Clark

"Don't know why there's no sun up in the sky."   Copernicus

"Is it soup yet?"   Andy Warhol

"Good things from the garden."   Timothy Leary

"I'll be a monkey's uncle."   William Jennings Bryan

"To make a long story short. . . ."   Marcel Proust

"How do I love thee? Let me count the ways."   Krafft-Ebbing

"Thank God it's Friday."   Robinson Crusoe

"Accuracy, accuracy, accuracy."   William Tell

"There is no tomorrow."   Hugh Downs

"He who enjoys his neighbor has a precious possession."   Bob,
   Carol, Ted, and Alice

". . . Never send to know for whom the bell tolls."   Pavlov

"A is for Apple."   Miss Hester Prynne

Wild Cards

Traditional wallet cards have been circulated for many years in printed form, and they continue to be found today in that medium. However, many of these cards are now copied and thus are actually paper. These paper "cards" or reproductions of cards serve the same purpose. There is no question that these wallet cards are a form of folklore, that is, they enjoy multiple existence (in space and time) and they demonstrate variation. Like all folklore, the wallet cards are passed on from individual to individual.

Of course, regular business or calling cards are in common use. Professionals and businessmen typically exchange cards upon a first meeting. They are a form of advertising and they may serve as a reminder of the meeting and a guarantee of spelling correctly the name and address of new contacts. The wallet cards reported here are humorous adaptations of staid formal business cards. These adaptations sometimes function as icebreakers. Salesmen, for example, may employ them to maintain goodwill with some customers.

Some wallet cards would fall under the rubric of membership or credit cards. In American society, cards are used to prove identity, provide evidence of membership in organizations, receive credit, and even literally open gates and doors. Cards are made of a variety of materials including cardboard and plastic. Membership and credit cards also have folkloristic analogues. It would be possible given the richness of the data to undertake a book-length study of traditional wallet cards. Here we are presenting only what we consider to be a representative sample.

A few items, including several of those from ISR, we have included for historical and comparative purposes. In some instances, we were unable to determine whether they circulate currently by copier means as do most of the wallet cards we have presented. We might observe that the gamut of materials found on wallet cards runs the entire range of copier urban folklore forms. Wordplay, double entendres, cartoons, and parodies, for example, are found individually and in combination on wallet cards. It was often a difficult decision to determine whether a given item should be reported in this section of the volume or in some other where it was equally appropriate. The important point is that wallet cards provide a microcosm of the total spectrum of urban folklore from the paperwork empire.

13. My Card

The first example was collected in Berkeley, California, in 1976. It plays on the conventional verbal formula uttered on the occasion of handing one's card to someone.

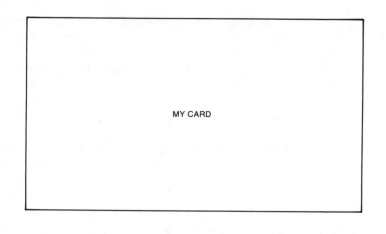

When You're up to Your Ass in Alligators . . .

14. My Card, Sir

This card could be presented to someone who was speaking. It might be used to interrupt a speaker or it might be passed to him after he had finished recounting some story. It is intended to impugn the credibility of the speaker. The first version was collected in Washington, D.C., in 1975. The second version, which we present to demonstrate the traditionality of the item, was collected in San Francisco in the early 1970s. For an English version, see OG2, 31.

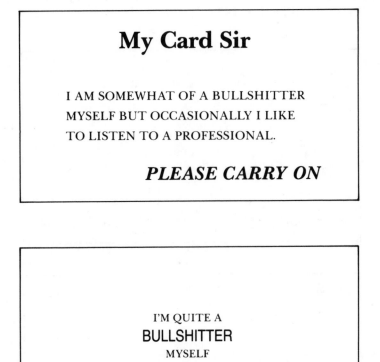

My Card Sir

I AM SOMEWHAT OF A BULLSHITTER
MYSELF BUT OCCASIONALLY I LIKE
TO LISTEN TO A PROFESSIONAL.

PLEASE CARRY ON

I'M QUITE A
BULLSHITTER
MYSELF
BUT GO AHEAD WITH YOUR STORY

15. Retired

One of the problems in American society is retirement in the sense that businessmen who retire sometimes feel worthless and forgotten. Because cards were a means of proving identity when businessmen were active, it is only natural to think of the absence of cards as a sign of inactivity. That the retiree's card may not even bear his name shows his feelings of anonymity and rejection. The card also underscores the normal accoutrements of business success: a phone, an address, money, and prospects. The first version was collected in San Francisco in 1973 from a retired gentleman who kept it in his wallet. The second version was collected in Oakland in 1975.

```
 no job                              no money



                 HARRY LIEBERMAN
                     retired



 no phone                           no address
```

```
 NO PHONE                          NO ADDRESS




                    Retired




 NO BUSINESS                       NO MONEY
 NO WORRIES                        NO PROSPECTS
```

When You're up to Your Ass in Alligators . . .

16. Sorry I Missed You!

Sometimes the client is not in when a salesman calls. To avoid wasting the visit, the salesman may leave a calling card. In this parody, the reference is to convicted mass murderer Juan Corona, who was accused of killing more than twenty migrant farm workers.

Sorry I missed you!

JUAN V. CORONA
Farm Labor Contractor

Yuba City, Calif.

17. While You Were Out

A client's secretary or answering service may be charged with recording visits by salesmen and other business callers. There are standard forms for such messages. This parody is not of a wallet card but of a common telephone message slip. The first item was collected in the Department of Anthropology at the University of California, Berkeley, in 1974. The second was collected at a government research installation near Knoxville, Tennessee, in 1977.

Date_____Time_____

WHILE YOU WERE OUT

M _____

Phone _____

| Telephoned | | Will call again | | Left package | |
| Please call | | Was in | | Left country | |

has	wants		quantity	price
☐	☐	marijuana		
☐	☐	hashish		
☐	☐	cocaine		
☐	☐	lsd		
☐	☐	mescaline		
☐	☐	psilocybin		

Message _____

_____

_____

_____

_____

CALL REPORT

Date _____ 19 ____

TELEPHONE CALL		PERSONAL CALL	
A.M.	P.M.	A.M.	P.M.

For Mr. _____

While you were . . .

☐ Drinking Coffee   ☐ Helling Around
☐ At the Beer Joint   ☐ On the Can
☐ Asleep   ☐ Tight   ☐ Mingling

Your . . .

☐ Wife   ☐ Blonde   ☐ Pal
☐ Bookie   ☐ Banker   ☐ Bootlegger
☐ Secretary   ☐ Broker   ☐ Red Head
☐ Mother-in-law   ☐ Probation Officer

Called and left word for you to . . .

☐ Bring some "B" girls along
☐ Send out that gallon of Bourbon
☐ Marry the girl
☐ Come by the Apartment
☐ Send check   ☐ Pay _____
☐ Renew that note
☐ Her husband came home
☐ Get the hell out of town

18. Complaint Form

The conclusion of a sale does not necessarily terminate the relationship between customer and seller. The buyer may have a complaint because of defective merchandise or because the merchandise is not suitable for the purpose intended. Sellers are never anxious to receive complaints from customers, but, on the other hand, they realize that it is in their best interest to hear and remedy legitimate complaints to maintain good customer relations. A spate of recent consumer legislation has imposed legal duties on many sellers of various products requiring them to honor commitments made at the time of sales. Most department stores have complaint windows and most large companies have customer relations specialists. The following item, collected in Oakland, California, in 1973, is a parody of the complaint form. The use of the pickle design might refer either to the colloquial "pickle" meaning an awkward or difficult situation or to the notion of "pickle-puss" suggesting the complainant is a sour and disagreeable person. (For another version—without the pickle motif—see YD, 105.)

19. Thanks for Taking Two Parking Places

Driving a car presents one set of problems, but finding a parking place in crowded cities presents another. The following card collected in Indianapolis in 1976 allows someone to complain anonymously about another individual's poor parking. Parking is a major problem for most urban Americans, and there are not many outlets for the expression of anger and frustration about this matter. (For another version, see YD, 83. For a German variant, see IK, 112.)

THANKS

FOR TAKING TWO PARKING PLACES

Due to your clumsy, careless way of parking,
I had to park three blocks out of my way.

You Stupid, Inconsiderate

BASTARD

20. Your Story Has Touched My Heart

Complaints in American culture may take the form of a hard luck story. Sometimes even a friend has to grit his teeth in listening to all the details of a long tale of woe. The following card provides a light response to such a tale, a response playing on the sympathy card customarily sent to a bereaved family. Implicit is the contrast between the genuine sorrow involved in a death and the pretended sorrow offered as a response to the hard luck story. The card was collected in the San Francisco Bay area in the early 1970s.

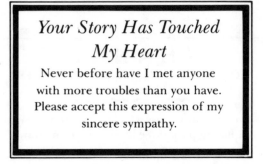

Your Story Has Touched My Heart
Never before have I met anyone with more troubles than you have. Please accept this expression of my sincere sympathy.

21. Sympathy Card

A much more direct (although alphabetically inaccurate) response to a hard luck story is the following card collected in Indianapolis in 1976.

IF YOU'RE LOOKING FOR

SYMPATHY

YOU'LL FIND IT IN THE DICTIONARY

BETWEEN **SHIT** *AND* **SUICIDE**

22. T. S. Card

The folk expression perhaps best summarizing a total lack of sympathy with a complainant is "tough shit," sometimes abbreviated T. S. Going back at least to World War II is the idea of a T. S. card, which could be offered to a complainant with the invitation to punch the appropriate portion as a means of registering his complaint or grievance. One such card on file at ISR, dating from 1945, was in use at the Naval Training School at Purdue University.

OFFICIAL T. S. CARD

ISSUED TO ....

☆ Guard Duty	*NOT TRANSFERABLE*	P.O. ☆
☆ Hang Over	*Punch out Star opposite each complaint*	Just Sad ☆
☆ Broke	*See Chaplain if possible*	No Date ☆
☆ No Mail	*Signed;*	Stood Up ☆
☆ Under Age —No Beer		Snafu ☆
		No Nookey ☆
☆ Married	*Approved;*	Restricted ☆
☆ No Leave		Extra Duty ☆
☆ A. O. L.		Captain's
☆ Brig		Mast ☆

BOTTOM LINE RESERVED FOR BROWN NOSING THAT DIDN'T WORK

23. The Three Most Overrated Things in the World

Much American humor is based on the superlative degree of comparison. For example, there is a popular oral formula that takes the form "What's (or Who's) the ——— est thing in the world?" An illustration is: What's the quietest thing in the world? A mosquito urinating on a blotter. (For other examples, see Alan Dundes and Robert A. Georges, "Some Minor Genres of Obscene Folklore," *Journal of American Folklore* 75 (1962): 223–24.) In ethnic humor, we find various answers to the question "What are the three shortest books in the world?", including: *Italian War Heroes, Jewish Business Ethics*, and *The Polish Mind*. (For an extended discussion of ethnic and national stereotypes in folklore, see Alan Dundes, "Slurs International: Folk Comparisons of Ethnicity and National Character," *Southern Folklore Quarterly* 39 (1975): 15–38.) In UFFC-TB, 163, we find an interesting version of "The Complete Library of the World's Smallest Books." The titles are: *Who's Who in Puerto Rico, The Complete Guide to Jewish Business Ethics, Irish Intellectuals, Italian War Heroes, An Outline of English Humor, Negro Business Leaders, Basics of Polish Hygiene, La Dolce Vita in Scotland*, and *Democracy in Germany*.

The following card collected in 1945 in San Francisco belongs to the same "superlatives" tradition. In this case, it is not an ethnic slur but a regional slur in which San Franciscans of northern California can express their long-standing rivalry with Los Angeles in southern California.

The Three Most
Over-rated Things
in the World:

1. *Home Cooking*
    2. *Home Screwing*
        3. *Los Angeles*

---

24. The Perfect Woman

The male stereotype of the ideal woman is that she should be a passive sex object. In this cartoon found in the wallet card format—it also occurs as a full-fledged cartoon—we find woman depicted as headless. This surely suggests that she should be silent and mindless. The male redrawing of female anatomy reveals a projection of male concerns for breasts and buttocks. The card was collected in Washington, D.C., in 1976.

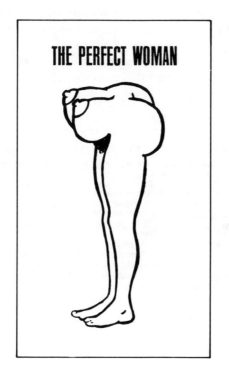

25. The Proposition Is This

Evidence attesting to the circulation of humorous wallet cards in the 1940s if not the 1930s is provided by the following versions of a series of sexually suggestive occupational double entendres. The prices evoke memories of a time long gone. When was the last time a person paid two or three dollars for a doctor's house call? For that matter, when was the last time a doctor made a house call?

The first version from San Francisco has an unusual drawing; when turned upside down, a man's smiling face is replaced by a sad or unhappy one. The second version from ISR has some content in common with the first but also has some that is different. The third version, collected in Kokomo, Indiana, in 1976, shows marked similarities to the versions from the 1940s. The variation in titles of the three versions is noteworthy.

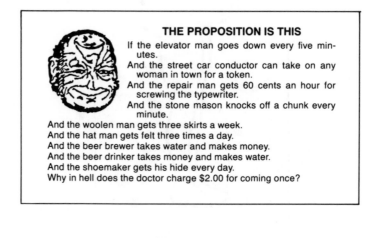

THE PROPOSITION IS THIS

If the elevator man goes down every five minutes.

And the street car conductor can take on any woman in town for a token.

And the repair man gets 60 cents an hour for screwing the typewriter.

And the stone mason knocks off a chunk every minute.

And the woolen man gets three skirts a week.

And the hat man gets felt three times a day.

And the beer brewer takes water and makes money.

And the beer drinker takes money and makes water.

And the shoemaker gets his hide every day.

Why in hell does the doctor charge $2.00 for coming once?

When You're up to Your Ass in Alligators . . .

If and Why

If a hat manufacturer gets his felt twice a year,
And a leather dealer gets his hide Tuesday and Thursday,
And an ice box gets a piece every morning,
And a table cloth gets jerked off three times a day,
And a street car conductor will take on any woman in town for a
    dime,
And the boss had to get in the stenographer's drawers to get lead
    in his pencil,
And a mechanic has to screw the typewriter while a dentist puts
    his tool in a woman's mouth for fifty cents,
Then why in the hell does a doctor charge $3.00 for coming once?

The Question Arises

If a Tailor lines three shirts a day,
And a hat factory gets felt every Tuesday and Thursday,
And an ice box gets a piece every morning,
And the table cloth gets jerked off three times a day,
And a Dentist gets fifty cents for putting his tool in a woman's
    mouth,
And a Ford gets its nuts tightened once a month,
And the ladies feel the Grocer's prunes for nothing,
Then why in the Hell does a Doctor charge three dollars for com-
    ing once!

26. You Have Insulted a Woman

The women's liberation movement of the 1970s fought the stereotype of the passive female who is ordered to submit to the demands of an aggressive male. To do this, women are being urged to strike back. The image of the militant feminist appears to some males as a threatening, perhaps castrating, figure. The following card, which was originally enclosed in a protective plastic covering, was collected in Columbus, Ohio, from a woman. Although the card could be passed from one male to another as a joke, it obviously has much more effect when given to a man by a woman.

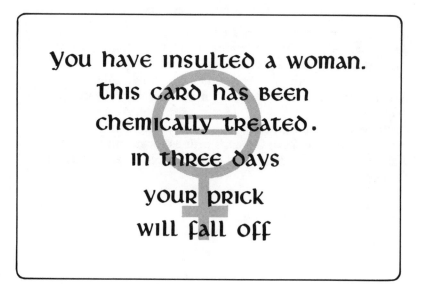

You have insulted a woman.
This card has been
chemically treated.
In three days
your prick
will fall off

27. The Turtle Club

Turtle Club membership cards are widely found throughout the United States. The cards reflect an initiation ritual that has been reported by folklorists. See Richard Bauman, "The Turtles: An American Riddling Institution," *Western Folklore* 29 (1970): 21–24. The rules printed on the back of the Turtle card give most of the salient details of the ritual.

The functioning of Turtles is of interest. Because a member is theoretically required to answer the question "Are you a Turtle?" wherever and whenever it is asked, one strategy is to direct the question to a known Turtle when he is either far away and/or in the middle of a crowd of non-Turtles. If he fulfills his ritual obligation, he must yell out, "You bet your sweet ass I am" in what might be an embarrassing context. Bauman reminds us that one of the astronauts on board the Apollo 7 spacecraft in 1968 asked a member of the ground control group, "Are you a turtle?" In this case, a considerable media audience could have heard or overhead the traditional response. The ground control project member answered, "I have recorded my answer" after having briefly switched off his microphone!

The induction of a new member of the Turtle Club may produce similar embarrassment because of the pretended obscene riddles that constitute the heart of the initiation tasks. The riddles force the initiate (and others present) to think of obscenities, and it is almost impossible for the uninitiated to conceive of any answer other than the obvious obscene one. We might observe that different pretended obscene riddles can be used in other versions of the Turtle ritual. Besides the riddles included on the card presented, there are the following two alternatives: (1) What goes in hard and comes out soft? (or What goes in long and hard and comes out soft and sticky?) Gum. (2) What is at the bottom of a bird cage and rhymes with mitt (or it)? Grit. Sometimes three rather than four riddles are asked.

As for why the name "Turtle" was selected, it is difficult to say. Possibly the phallic significance of a turtle's head as it emerges from its shell could explain the turtle's association with a group of pretended obscene riddles. The pajama riddle, for example, is not dissimilar in its metaphor to the protrusion of a turtle's head.

The card presented here was collected in Los Angeles in 1968. (For a version from England involving the Interstellar Association of Turtles, Outershell Division, see TCB, 78.)

International Association of

TURTLES

Date_____

THIS IS TO CERTIFY THAT

_____

IS A MEMBER IN GOOD STANDING AND WILL REMAIN SO AS LONG AS HE CONTINUES TO GIVE THE PASSWORD WHEN ASKED BY A FELLOW TURTLE.

IMPERIAL TURTLE

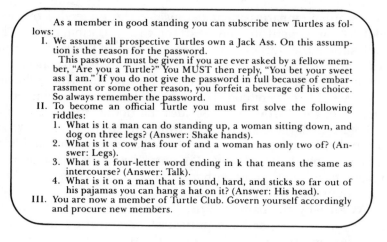

As a member in good standing you can subscribe new Turtles as follows:

I. We assume all prospective Turtles own a Jack Ass. On this assumption is the reason for the password.

This password must be given if you are ever asked by a fellow member, "Are you a Turtle?" You MUST then reply, "You bet your sweet ass I am." If you do not give the password in full because of embarrassment or some other reason, you forfeit a beverage of his choice. So always remember the password.

II. To become an official Turtle you must first solve the following riddles:

1. What is it a man can do standing up, a woman sitting down, and dog on three legs? (Answer: Shake hands).
2. What is it a cow has four of and a woman has only two of? (Answer: Legs).
3. What is a four-letter word ending in k that means the same as intercourse? (Answer: Talk).
4. What is it on a man that is round, hard, and sticks so far out of his pajamas you can hang a hat on it? (Answer: His head).

III. You are now a member of Turtle Club. Govern yourself accordingly and procure new members.

When You're up to Your Ass in Alligators . . .

28. How Do You Keep a Polack Occupied for a Year?

This card is part of the larger Polack joke cycle. (For a discussion of this cycle, see Alan Dundes, "A Study of Ethnic Slurs: The Jew and the Polack in the United States," *Journal of American Folklore* 84 [1971]: 186–203.) The joke cycle has inspired a number of catches. For example, someone tells the dupe that the joke cycle has become so popular that there is now a dial-a-Polack joke telephone number in every city in the United States, a service like Dial-a-Prayer, and so forth. The number is easy to remember: POLLACQ. The following item was collected in Berkeley in 1976.

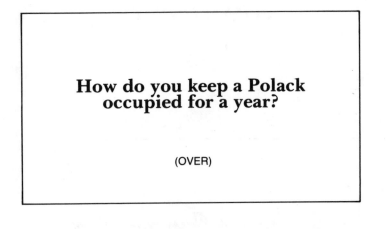

How do you keep a Polack occupied for a year?

(OVER)

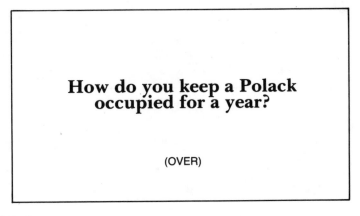

How do you keep a Polack occupied for a year?

(OVER)

29. I'd Rather Do Business

Another ethnic joke found in the wallet card tradition involves Arabs and Jews. This version was collected in Washington, D.C., in 1976.

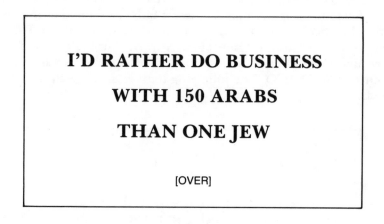

When You're up to Your Ass in Alligators . . .

30. Let's Analyze the Weather

Folk poetry appears in all forms of copier folklore. Wallet cards are no exception. This poem in ISR was collected in Bloomington, Indiana, in 1961, on a card bearing the name of a printer in Taylorville, Illinois.

"LET'S ANALYZE THE WEATHER"

When summer comes we have a dread,
   Cause the weather's hot and sultry;
We drag around as though half dead,
   Tis no time for adultery.

Then comes fall in late November.
   When the frost is on the pumpkin;
And all of a sudden, we remember,
   That's the time for Peter Dunkin!

One can compare the text with a verse collected by Vance Randolph from an informant in Elk Creek, Missouri, in December 1949. (See Vance Randolph, "Vulgar Rhymes from the Ozarks," manuscript [1954] on file in ISR, 222.)

When the dew is on the lily
Then the Ozark hilly-billy
Is scratching ticks and chiggers all the day,
But when the frost is on the punkin
That's time for peter dunkin'
With his wife knocked up, and crops all
   laid away.

31. Revised Miranda

Ever since the celebrated United States Supreme Court case of *Miranda v. Arizona* in 1966, law enforcement officers have been required to advise accused individuals of their rights at the time of arrest. Typical features of the Miranda warning include: You have the right to remain silent; anything you say may be used against you. You have the right to be represented by counsel of your choice. If you cannot afford counsel of your choice, one will be appointed for you. This parody was collected at the campus police station of the University of California, Berkeley, in 1976.

REVISED MIRANDA

You have the right to swing first. However
if you choose to swing first, any move you
make can and will be used as an excuse to
beat the shit out of you. You have the
right to have a doctor and a priest present.
If you cannot afford a doctor or are not
presently attending a church of your choice,
one will be appointed for you.
Do you understand what I just told you,
asshole?

Those Cards and Letters

The category of cards includes more than merely wallet cards. Cards used in correspondence such as greeting cards are also well represented in copier folklore. From greeting cards we move to traditional letters. We presented some twenty traditional letters in UF, but this did not exhaust the repertoire by any means. We have included another few specimens here.

For many years, conventional commercial greeting cards tended to restrict their content to a small set of saccharine, hackneyed formulaic phrases. In recent times, there has been a noticeable trend toward lighter and more humorous greetings—some even bordering on antigreetings. The folk have long enjoyed disrespectful and in some instances downright insulting parodies of the standard language of seasonal greetings.

32. Doing a Little Business

Although not recorded in many American slang dictionaries, the word *business* can refer to feces. A house pet, for example, might be described as having "done his business on the carpet." The business = feces equation may strike some readers as being bizarre, but if one remembers that business is clearly concerned with making money and that money and feces are often symbolic equivalents, the association is not really so strange. (Evidence for the money-feces symbology in American folk speech includes such expressions as filthy or stinking rich, to be rolling in it, to make one's pile, or to have money up the ass. Similarly, the expression for payday among federal employees; "the day the eagle flies over" or "the day the eagle shits," provides another unambiguous example. For other folkloristic data, see Sigmund Freud and D. E. Oppenheim, *Dreams in Folklore* (New York: International Universities Press, 1958) and Legman, NLM, 917–20.)

The following pseudogreeting card is from ISR and was collected in Washington, D.C., in 1947. It is a marvelous example of a literalization of a metaphor.

GREETINGS

DOING A LITTLE BUSINESS
ON A LARGE SCALE

33. I Had Twelve Bottles

Progressive intoxication is the premise responsible for the compositional technique of the following classic account. Although the account is sometimes recited in oral tradition, it is also common in copier tradition. Our first version dates from 1940 in Cedar Rapids, Iowa, and it is almost identical to other versions circulating in the 1970s. We have presented a second version from Concord, New Hampshire, in 1977, to show just how stable the tradition has been for nearly forty years. A third version, collected in northern Indiana in 1967, shows some variation. It has apparently incorporated some short one-liners about drinking.

I had twelve bottles of spirits in my cellar and my wife told me to empty the contents of each bottle or else!

So I said I would and proceeded with my unpleasant task.

I withdrew the cork from the first bottle and poured the contents down the sink—with the exception of one glass which I drank. I then withdrew the cork from the second bottle and did likewise—with the exception of one glass which I drank. I extracted the cork from the third bottle and poured the whiskey down the cork from the fourth sink and poured the bottle down the glass which I drank. I pulled the bottle from the cork out of the next and drank one sink out of it and threw the rest down the glass. I pulled a sink out of the next glass and poured one cork from the bottle then I corked the sink with the glass, bottled the drink and drank the pour. When I had everything emptied I steadied the house with one hand counted the bottles, corks, glasses, and sinks with the other which were 29, and as the house came by I counted them again and finally had all the houses and bottles and corks and glasses and sinks counted except one house and one bottle which I drank.

I had twelve bottles of whiskey in my cellar and my wife told me to empty the contents of each and every bottle down the sink, or else, so I said that I would, and I proceeded with the first bottle and poured the contents down the sink with the exception of one glass which I drank. I extracted the cork from the second bottle and likewise, with the exception of one glass which I drank. I withdrew the cork from the third bottle and poured the good booze down the sink, except one glass which I drank. I then pulled the bottle from the cork of the next and drank one sink from it and poured the rest down the glass. I pulled the sink out of the next glass and poured the cork down the bottle. I pulled the next cork out of my throat and poured the sink down the bottle and drank the glass. I corked the sink with the next bottle and drank the pour. When I had emptied everything I steadied the house with one hand and counted the bottles, corks, and glasses with the other, which was twenty-nine. To be sure I counted them again when they came by me, and I had seventy-four. And as the sink came by me and the bottles and the pours I counted them again, and finally I had all the houses and bottles and corks and glasses counted, except one bottle and one house which I drank.

A friend of mine gave me ten little bottles of some special stuff that he brewed up hisself. . . .

I took it and hid it down in my basement.

But my wife found out about it and told me to get rid of it or else. . . .

Since I didn't like the way she said "or else" . . . I went down there and proceeded to carry out her instructions.

I set the ten little bottles on the drain board. Picked up the first bottle . . . pulled the cork out of it and poured it down the sink . . . all except one little swaller . . . which I drank.

I picked up the next bottle and I pulled the sink out of it . . . and I poured it . . . down the sink
All except one little swaller . . . which I drank.

I picked up the next cork, and I pulled the sink out of it and I poured it down the bottle . . . all except one little swaller . . . which I sank.

I used to have a great deal of difficulty with this number. You see, I come from a great long line of stinkers . . . er, drinkers. . . .

I had an uncle who drank a quart a day every day of his life. No kiddin' he could drink a quart and not even stagger . . . he couln' even move.

The doctor said you'd better quit drinkin' that stuff, It's gonna kill ya. . . . Sure enough it killed him. He died last year at the age of a hundred and two.

Ya know, we dug him up last week, and he looks better than ya'll do now . . . A man asked me what's the difference between a drunk and a alcoholic . . . well, I'll tell ya . . . us drunks don't have to attend all those daggone meetings.

I want you to know one little thing . . . you better not say nothin' about me wife, buster . . . 'cause I want ya to know I got the wicest little kife in the whole United States.

Several versions nearly identical with the first two above had a different final paragraph. For example, a version entitled "Twelve Bottles" collected in Costa Mesa, California, in 1976, ended as follows: "I'm not under the alcofluence of incohol, but thinkle peep I am. I'm not half so thunk as you might drink. I fool so feelish—I don't know who is me and the frunker I stand here the longer I get." This paragraph is a borrowing from the standard folk parody of "Twinkle, Twinkle, Little Star," which goes as follows:

> Starkle starkle little twink
> Who the hell you are I think.
> I'm not under the alcofluence of incohol
> I'm not as drunk as some thinkle peep I am
> And besides I only had tea Martoonies
> Anyway I've all day Sober to sunday up in
> I fool so feelish I don't know who is me yet
> But the drunker I stand here the longer I get.

34. Dear First Born

Sibling rivalry is a fact of family life and probably cannot be avoided. However, parents ideally are expected not to show favoritism to any one of their children. At least this is so in modern times in the United States, where primogeniture is not in effect. At the same time, parents often try to make each child feel special and different from his or her siblings. This is a difficult and delicate task. Birth order is significant and surely has an effect on the development of individual personalities. The following text collected in Palo Alto, California, in 1977, offers in letter format a folk solution to the perennial problem of how to treat each child.

Dear First Born:

I've always loved you best because you were our first miracle. You were the genesis of a marriage and the fulfillment of young love.

You sustained us through the hamburger years, the first apartment (furnished in Early Poverty), our first mode of transportation (1955 feet) and the 7-inch TV we paid on for 36 months.

You were new and had unused grandparents and enough clothes for a set of triplets. You were the original model for a mom and a dad who were trying to work the bugs out. You got the strained lamb, the open safety pins and three-hour naps.

You were the beginning.

Dear Middle Child:

I've always loved you best because you drew a tough spot in the family and it made you stronger for it.

You cried less, had more patience, wore faded hand-me downs and never in your life did anything first. But it only made you more special. You were the one we relaxed with and realized a dog could kiss you and you wouldn't get sick. You could cross a street by yourself long before you were old enough to get married. And you helped us understand the world wouldn't collapse if you went to bed with dirty feet.

You were the child of our busy ambitious years. Without you we never could have survived the job changes and the tedium and routine that is marriage.

To The Baby:

I've always loved you best because while endings are generally sad, you are such a joy. You readily accepted the milk-stained bibs, the lower bunk, the cracked baseball bat, the baby book that had nothing written in it except a recipe for graham-cracker piecrust that someone had jammed between the pages.

You are the one we held onto so tightly. You are the link with our past, a reason for tomorrow. You quicken our steps, square our shoulders, restore our vision and give us a sense of humor that security, maturity and durability can't provide.

When your hairline takes on the shape of Lake Erie and your own children tower over you, you will still be our baby.

Mom

35. Benjamin Franklin's Advice to a Young Man in Love

This classic letter is included in *The Papers of Benjamin Franklin* published by Yale University Press. Because the letter is indisputably still in folk tradition, we have here a letter that has circulated for more than two hundred years. It is known under a variety of titles: "Advice to a Young Man on the Choice of a Mistress," "A Letter on Marriage," "Old Mistresses Apologue." Three versions were found among the papers inherited by William Temple Franklin from his illustrious grandfather. One was in Franklin's own hand and another copy contained additions made by Franklin. The existence of more than one version plus a tiny fragment in French (also in Franklin's hand) suggest either that the letter went immediately into tradition or that Franklin used a letter already in English (or French) tradition.

Because of its content, the letter was effectively suppressed—at least officially—for nearly two centuries. Although occasionally issued in private limited editions or through underground printings, the letter did not reach the wider general public until its first open mass publication in 1926. By 1941 the letter appeared in *Treasury of the World's Great Letters*, which was available as a Book-of-the-Month Club dividend.

This is not the only controversial piece attributed to Franklin. The frequently reprinted "Speech of Miss Polly Baker," which purports to be a plea before the court for an unwed mother of five children, is reportedly another Franklin creation. (In some versions, she later marries and bears fifteen more children!) For a fascinating account of this tradition, see Max Hall, *Benjamin*

Franklin and Polly Baker: The History of a Literary Deception (Chapel Hill: University of North Carolina Press, 1960). For a useful account of the complex history of "Advice to a Young Man in Love," see Leonard W. Labaree, ed., *The Papers of Benjamin Franklin*, vol. 3 (New Haven: Yale University Press, 1961), pp. 27–31. For "The Speech of Miss Polly Baker," see pp. 120–25. For details of another jeu d'esprit, "A Parable against Persecution," which Franklin pretended was a chapter of Genesis in which Abraham is allegedly punished by God for failing to grant hospitality to a passing unbeliever, see vol. 6 (New Haven: Yale University Press, 1963), pp. 114–24.

Modern versions of "Advice" continue to show minor variations in diction and punctuation. Many contain introductory explanations claiming to account for the existence of the letter. These initial explanations also manifest considerable diversity. The version presented here is from the ISR folklore file and it was collected in Chicago in 1959. (Another version in ISR, supposedly printed in North Carolina, was collected in 1973.) A version also appeared under the title "Franklin on Marriage" in *Over Sexteen* (New York: Elgart, 1951), pp. 88–89.

As for Franklin's concluding remark that older women are grateful for sexual favors, a modern memorandum makes much the same point. A version that circulated at the Mare Island Naval Shipyard in Vallejo, California, in 1968, goes as follows:

> I like women over forty . . .
>   they don't tell—
>   they don't yell—
>   they don't swell—
>   and they're grateful as hell!

(For another text, see *More Over Sexteen* [New York: Grayson, 1953], p. 121.)

A YOUNG MAN having entered a profession poor, without visible means to support a wife, and being of a very amorous temperament, was in grave doubt as to the best means for him to pursue in conducting his amours. After deep thought upon the matter, WITHOUT ARRIVING AT A SATISFACTORY SOLUTION OF THE SUBJECT, he concluded to appeal to a friend—the greatest of all philosophers of his time—BENJAMIN FRANKLIN. The following letter is one of those written by Mr. Franklin in answer to the inquiries of the young gentleman.

        When You're up to Your Ass in Alligators . . .

The original of the letter is in the possession and is the property of the United States Government, and can be found at Washington among the unpublished correspondence of Benjamin Franklin, recently purchased by the Government.

June 25th, 1745.

My Dear Friend:—

I know of no medicine fit to diminish the violent nocturnal inclinations you mention, and if I did, I think I should not communicate it to you. Marriage is the proper remedy. It is the most natural state of man, and, therefore, the state in which you are most likely to find solid happiness. Your reasons against entering it at present appear to me not well founded. The circumstantial advantages you have in view of postponing it are not only uncertain, but they are small in comparison with that of the thing itself—The being married and settled.

It is the man and woman united that make the complete human being. Separate, she wants his force of body and strength of reason; he her softness, sensibility and acute discernment. Together they are more likely to succeed in the world. A single man has not nearly the value he would have in a state of union. He is an incomplete animal. He resembles the odd half of a pair of scissors. If you get a prudent, healthy wife, your industry in your profession, and with her good economy, will be a fortune sufficient.

But if you will not take this counsel, and persist in thinking a commerce with the sex inevitable, then I repeat my former advice, that in your amours you should prefer old women to young ones. You call this a paradox and demand my reasons. They are these:

First—Because they have more knowledge of the world, and their minds are better stored with observations; their conversation is more improving and more lastingly agreeable.

Second—Because when women cease to be handsome they study to be good. To maintain their influence over men they supply the diminution of beauty by an augmentation of utility. They learn to do a thousand services, small and great, and are the most tender and useful of all friends when you are sick. Thus they continue amiable, and hence there is scarcely such a thing to be found as an old woman who is not a good woman.

Third—Because there is no hazard of children, which, irregularly produced, may be attended with much inconvenience.

Fourth—Because though more experienced, they are more prudent and discreet in conducting an intrigue to prevent suspicion. The commerce with them is therefore safe with regard to your reputation, and, with regard to theirs, if the affair should happen to be known, considerate people might be rather inclined to excuse an old woman who would kindly take care of a young man, form his manners by her good counsels, and prevent his ruining his health and fortune among mercenary prostitutes.

Fifth—Because in every animal that walks upright the deficiency of the fluid that fills the muscles appears but on the highest part. The face first grows lank and wrinkled—then the neck, then the breast and arms—the lower parts continuing to the last as plump as ever; so that covering all above with a basket and regarding only what is below the girdle, it is impossible of two women to know an old from a young one. And as in the dark all cats are grey, the pleasure of corporal enjoyment with an old woman is at least equal and frequently superior; every knack being, by practice, capable of improvement.

Sixth—Because the sin is less. The debauching a virgin may be her ruin, and make her life unhappy.

Seventh—Because the compunction is less. The having made a young girl miserable may give you frequent bitter reflections, none of which can attend the making of an old woman happy.

Eighth, and lastly. They are so grateful.
This much for my paradox, but I still advise you to marry immediately, being sincerely

Your affectionate friend,
B. Franklin.

When You're up to Your Ass in Alligators . . .

36. Automobile Accident Insurance Claims

The attempt to reduce the complexities of human life situations to facile paperwork formats, for example, in the insurance business, has encouraged ingenuity in filling out these forms. The pervasive requirements of fitting one's needs into a priori fixed categories to qualify for benefits has produced a colorful variety of justifications of behavior. The following list circulated at the California Traffic Safety Foundation in Oakland in 1974. (For English versions, see YWIW, [17]; OG2, 4; and TCB, 143–44. For another version, see YD, 12.) Its compositional technique, though not its content, is like that employed in the list of sentences supposedly taken from welfare applications or from excuses for school absences reported in UF, 140–43.

WOULD YOU BELIEVE?

Here are how motorists explain a car crash in submitting an insurance claim to Allstate:

To avoid a collision, I ran into the other car.

I blew my horn, but it wouldn't work as it was stolen.

Car had to turn sharper than was necessary, owing to an invisible truck.

A pedestrian hit me and went under my car.

I knocked over a man. He admitted it was his fault as he had been run over before.

The other man altered his mind, so I had to run over him.

I left my car unattended for a minute, when by accident, or design, it ran away.

I collided with a stationary bus coming the other way.

I can give no details of the accident as I was somewhat concussed at the time.

Coming home I drove into the wrong house and collided with a tree I don't have.

37. Commuter's Complaint

This item, collected in Los Altos, California, in 1968, consists of an exchange of letters rather than a single letter. The issue in question concerns mass transit. The biblical reference in the final letter is inaccurate—there is no "Chapter of David." But there are biblical references to persons riding asses, for example, Zech. 9:9, John 12:15. The inaccuracy scarcely diminishes the effect of the final response. For a 1951 version of this item set in Philadelphia rather than Chicago, see *Over Sexteen* (New York: Elgart, 1951), p. 125.

The Chicago Surface Lines received the following letter from a disgruntled car rider who lives on the outskirts of the city.

Chicago Surface Lines   March 20, 1940
Chicago, Ill.

I have been riding your cars for the last ten years and the service seems to be worse every day. In fact, I think that the transportation you offer is not as good as that enjoyed by the people a thousand years ago.

> Yours truly
>
> John A. Smith
> 12365 S Western Ave.
> Chicago, Ill.

To this letter the Chicago Surface Lines made the following reply:

Mr. John A. Smith
Chicago, Ill.

Dear Sir:

We have your letter of the 20th, and believe you are somewhat confused in your history. The only transportation a thousand years ago was traveling on foot.

> Yours truly
> Chicago Surface Lines

To this letter Mr. Smith sent the following reply:

Chicago Surface Lines
Chicago, Ill.

Gentlemen:

I am in receipt of your letter of March 22nd. and think that you are the ones who are confused in your history. If you will read the Bible Chapter of David, 8th. Verse, you will find that Aaron rode into town on his ass more than a thousand years ago. That is something I have been unable to do on your street cars in the past ten years!

Yours truly

John A. Smith

38. Rejection Letter from *Playgirl*

One of the results of the women's liberation movement has been to put traditional male criteria for judging female worth into a new perspective. The American male penchant for rating women on the basis of body measurements, e.g., bust, waist, hips, has been criticized. Women without the requisite physical features were often rejected out of hand by males in authority.

The beauty contest mentality is applied in reverse to the male oppressor in the following popular folk letter. Most versions do not have a postscript as does the text below collected in Storrs, Connecticut, in 1975. However, one version offered the following postscript: "P.S. It may be the distortion in the picture, but it appears that your nose is the largest thing on your body" while another contained in an English collection exclaimed, "PS We commend you for your unusual pose. Were you wounded in the war—or do you ride a bike a lot?" See TCB, 132.

The traditionality of the letter is strongly evidenced by variation. For example, letterheads on the versions in our corpus show addresses in Chicago, Los Angeles, and San Francisco, besides New York City. A San Francisco version is purportedly written by Carol Doda, a prominent local entertainer, who is not the editor of *Playgirl*.

PLAYGIRL, INC.

NEW YORK, NEW YORK 10021

Dear Sir:

We wish to thank you for your letter and pictures which we recently received. However, we will not be able to use your body in our centerfold.

On a scale from 0 to 10, your body was rated −2. The rating is done by a panel of women ranging in age from 65 to 75 years. We tried to have our panel of women in the 25 to 35 year old bracket rate you, but we could not get them to stop laughing long enough.

Should the taste of the American women ever change so drastically that they would want you in the centerfold, you will be notified by this office. In the meantime, however, don't call us, we'll call you.

Sympathetically,

Amanda Smith, Editor
Playgirl magazine

AS:lb

P.S. If you wish to resubmit any additional pictures of yourself, may we suggest you look into the possibility of "trick" photography which in your case could bring better results.

39. Cable from Ireland

Significant political events can quickly enter the folklore of a society. The tragic event at Chappaquiddick Island in Massachusetts in 1969, which resulted in the death of Mary Jo Kopechne, certainly adversely affected the career of Senator Edward Kennedy who drove the death vehicle off a bridge. A number of jokes were spawned by the incident. For example, Miss Kopechne repeatedly tries to say something to Senator Kennedy who replies each time, "Later, later." Finally, she says, "What if I'm pregnant?" He replies, "We'll cross that bridge when we come to it." Many Americans were ready to think the worst of Senator Kennedy because of the unexplained circumstances surrounding the event.

The following item of folklore posits the unwavering blind support of Irish Catholics for the Kennedy family regardless of the issue. It could also, of course, be construed as an arch comment on the difficulty in believing Senator Kennedy's own version of what happened. The first version was collected in San Francisco in 1971. The second version was collected in Concord, New Hampshire, in 1977.

At the time of the events at Chappaquiddick, the Irish Government was faced with something of a public dilemma, since the Irish people had such great reverence for the Kennedy family.

After much consideration, the government decided to comment via a diplomatic cable to the United States. The cable read as follows:

> "God bless Senator Kennedy, that sainted soul, who was taking that fine Catholic girl to midnight mass when the tragedy occurred. Noble man that he was, he remained at the scene of the accident for nine hours in devout prayer. The American Government would be well advised to find the Protestant bastards who built the bridge."

Dublin Dispatch
THE VOICE OF THE IRISH FREE WORLD

GOD SAVES SENATOR KENNEDY AS GIRL DROWNS

DEVOUT PAIR BELIEVED TO BE ON WAY TO MIDNIGHT MASS

TED PRAYS FOR ALMOST NINE HOURS BEFORE LEAVING ACCIDENT SCENE

IRISH GOVERNMENT BLAMES ITALIAN CONTRACTOR FOR FAULTY BRIDGE

When You're up to Your Ass in Alligators . . .

40. Strong Letter to Follow

The advent of cables and telegrams has to some extent replaced the older letter form as a means of effective communication between individuals separated by great distances. The telephone can be used but there are times when one wishes to send a message without wanting a response. Because one normally pays for telegrams on the basis of the number of words, there has developed a knack of composing succinct sentences. The following text collected in San Jose, California, in 1978, from an employee of Pacific Telephone Company, perhaps contains the kind of message many would like to send to an enemy but dare not. Its effect comes from its brevity and its profanity.

Class of Service	WESTERN UNION	SYMBOLS
This is a last message unless its deferred character be indicated by the proper symbol.	TELEGRAM	DL = Day Letter NL = Night Letter LT = International Letter Telegram

Send the following message, subject to the terms on back hereof, which are hereby agreed to

TO   CARE OF OR APT. NO.

STREET & NO.   TELEPHONE

CITY & STATE   ZIP CODE

FUCK YOU

STRONG LETTER TO FOLLOW

SENDER'S TEL. NO.   NAME & ADDRESS

41. Take a Letter

The relationship between bosses and secretaries can be affected by reciprocal misperceptions. Bosses complain about incompetent secretaries who cannot spell or type; secretaries are apprehensive about overly demanding bosses who fail to appreciate the considerable skill required to convert raw dictation into smooth copy. This item illustrates the boss's view of the stenographer as a mindless vehicle and the stenographer's view of the boss as a bumbling idiot. The sexual components of the stereotypes are also present: the secretary who pulls up her skirt and the boss who attempts to initiate a personal relationship by inviting a new girl for a drink or lunch. The secretary's fears of being unappreciated, being subjected to unwanted sexual advances, and ultimately of being fired are all expressed in the following text, which circulated in Cedar Rapids, Iowa, in the early 1940s.

"Now look here. I fired three girls for revising my letters, see?" said the boss to his new steno.

"Yes, sir."

"Alright; now take a letter and take it the way I tell you."

And the next morning Mr. O. J. Squizz of the Squizz Soap Company received the following letter:

"Mr. O. K. or A. J. or something, look it up, Squizz, what a name, Soap Company, Detroit, that's in Michigan, isn't it? Dear Mr. Squizz. Hmm. The last shipment of soap you sent us was of inferior quality and I want you to understand—no, scratch that out. I want you to understand—hmm—unless you can ship—furnish, ship, no furnish us with your regular soap you needn't ship us no more, period, or whatever the grammar is, and pull down your skirt!

Where was I? Paragraph. Your soap wasn't what you said—I should say it wasn't. Them bums tried to put over a lot of hooey on us. Whadda you want to paint yer faces up for like indians on the warpath. We're sending back your last shipment tomorrow. Sure, we're gonna send it back. I'd like to feed it to 'em with a spoon an' make 'em eat it, the bums. Now read it over, we've wasted enough times on them crooks, fix it up and sign my name. What do you say we go out to lunch."

42. Service Policy

There is an art to answering letters of complaint. Companies wish to maintain good rapport with customers but they must defend themselves diplomatically against criticism. The following popular business form letter shows what the seller would like to tell the complaining buyer but cannot. The version presented here was collected in Napa, California, in 1974.

SERVICE POLICY

In accordance with company policy, we are pleased to announce that you received merchandise with the same high quality standards offered all our customers, and we feel you are extremely chicken-shit on returning this stuff, particularly since we did not authorize the return.

You know damned well we have a comprehensive and equitable Returned Goods Policy, and you will pay hell receiving credit unless this policy is strictly adhered to.

We ship whatever the Hell comes off the production line, and regardless if it meets specifications or not is beside the point. We are reasonably confident our packaging contains the proper materials a good share of the time, which is exactly what you ordered. By God no one is perfect. I'd like to see your production area sometime. I'll bet you have a shit-pot full of problems too.

Incidentally, you have really pissed-off our Scheduling and Production people with your arbitrary statements regarding late delivery. After all, your order was only three months overdue, which is a helluva lot better than most of our customers get. What the hell do you expect?

On future orders, we suggest you favor us with a higher dollar volume, and we will bust our ass. With this type volume, we can guarantee a maximum late order condition of two months . . . how's that for a 30-day improvement?

As a valued customer, it is certainly your privilege to request we check future orders more closely for requested shipping dates, but your prickish attitude will, we are confident, result in our shipping so damned late you will be in such a bind that you will gladly accept any old shit we want to get rid of.

By the way, don't give us any crap about order cancellation; we're already in production. We could, however, see our way clear to stop production if you will pay 90% cancellation charges. Otherwise, tough shit.

In summary, you work with us, and we will work with you. BUT don't pull that irate customer shit on us; we've been down that path before.

Warm personal regards,

CUSTOMER SERVICE MANAGER

P.S. You screwed up again when you insisted our part doesn't resemble your specification drawing. BULLSHIT!! Your drawing isn't even close to our part. We knew there was 1¼" difference between the part and the drawing, which we consider minor and totally insignificant. Why don't you get on your engineer's ass for a change?

43. Not Raising Hogs

The dream of getting something for nothing frequently becomes reality through the largesse of government giveaway programs. Agricultural commodity price supports and subsidies are considered by many to be ideal examples of this philosophy. The following letter collected at Chabot College, Hayward, California, in 1971, pokes fun at government acreage allotment and price subsidy programs.

Dear Mr. Senator:

My friend Bordeaux over in Pima County received a $1,000 check from the Government this year for not raising hogs. So I am going into the not-raising-hogs business next year. What I want to know is, in your opinion, what is the best kind of hogs not to raise? I would prefer not to raise Razorbacks, but, if there is no other good breed to not raise, I will just as gladly not raise Berkshires or Durocs.

The hardest work in this business is going to be in keeping an inventory of how many hogs I haven't raised. My friend Bordeaux is very joyful about the future of this business. He has been raising hogs for more than 20 years and the best he ever made was $400 until this year, when he got $1,000 for not raising hogs. If I can get $1,000 for not raising 50 hogs, then I will get $2,000 for not raising 100 hogs.

I plan to operate on a small scale at first, holding myself down to about 4,000 hogs, which means I will have $80,000. Now, another thing: These hogs I will not raise will not eat 100,000 bushels of corn. I understand that you also pay farmers for not raising corn. So will you pay me anything for not raising 100,000 bushels of corn not to feed the hogs I am not raising? I want to get started as soon as possible as this seems to be a good time of the year for not raising hogs.

44. The Cat Ranch Investment

Part of the "something for nothing" philosophy is reflected in the multitude of "get rich quick" schemes. Would-be investors are deluged with invitations to participate in developments in oil wells, real estate, orange groves, livestock feedlots, mink farms, catfish ranches, and the like. The arguments invariably include high and fast return at little or no risk with huge tax advantages. The offer is typically described as a once-in-a-lifetime opportunity, which must be seized quickly or it will be forever lost. Sometimes the appeal of the scheme is based on some new invention, process, or concept analogous to building a better mousetrap. Incidentally, it is interesting that according to the fourteenth edition of Bartlett's *Familiar Quotations* the aphoristic phrase "If a man can . . . make a better mousetrap . . . the world will make a beaten path to his door" has been attributed to Ralph Waldo Emerson, though it does not appear in his printed works.

The following text was collected in Alameda, California, in 1975.

July 8, 1975

Dear ———:

This is of the utmost urgency. The following is the "sleeper" of all "sleepers." Please send your check in the amount of $50,000 immediately. We are limiting each participant to one unit. You can understand after reading this once in a life time offer.

A group of us are considering investing in a large cat ranch near Hermosillo, Mexico. It is our purpose to start rather small with about one million cats. Each cat averages about twelve kittens a year; skins can be sold for about 20¢ for the white one and up to 40¢ for the black. This will give us twelve million cat skins per year to sell at an average price of around 32¢, making our gross revenue about $3 million a year. This really averages out to about $10,000 a day, excluding Sundays and holidays.

A good Mexican cat man can skin about 50 cats each day, at a wage of $13.15 a day. It will take 663 men to operate the ranch, so the net profit would be over $8,200 per day. Your $50,000 investment would be recovered in 6.1 days, which beats the stock market.

Now, the cats would be fed on rats exclusively. Rats multiply four times as fast as cats. We would start a rat ranch adjacent to our cat farm. If we start with a million rats, we will have four rats per cat per day. The rats will be fed on the carcasses of the cats that we skin. This will give each rat a quarter of a cat. You can see by this that the business is a clean operation; self-supporting and really automatic throughout. The cats will eat the rats and the rats will eat the cats and we will get the skins.

Eventually, it is our hope to cross the cats with snakes, for they will skin themselves twice a year. This would save the labor cost of skinning, as well as give us two skins for one cat.

Time is of the essence. Any hesitation on your part would be sheer disaster.

Become a millionaire with us through knowledgeable investments.

Sincerely,

When You're up to Your Ass in Alligators . . .

P.S. Somehow the word got out, so we had to buy 1 million snakes before the price went up. Please enclose a check for $10.00 to cover your share of this purchase.

YOU REALIZE, OF COURSE, THAT WHEN WE GET INTO OPERATION WE WILL HAVE THE BIGGEST CAT HOUSE IN THE WORLD AND OUR CLIENTELE WILL COME FROM ALL OVER TO BUY OUR PRODUCT.

The Writing on the Walls:
Notices, Mottoes, and Awards

Many of the items of urban folklore presented thus far are kept in the personal possession of individuals. They may be passed around or sent surreptitiously, but they are not necessarily posted on bulletin boards. There is, however, a vast array of notices, memoranda, and mottoes prominently displayed in offices under plastic or glass desktops or on walls, filing cabinets, or bulletin boards. Most of these materials tend to be philosophical and depend less on obscenity for their effect, probably because they are commonly displayed for public view. The public exposure of these materials makes them a good deal easier to collect than some other forms of urban folklore. Some of these materials have been exploited commercially. For example, many folk mottoes are sold in plaque or card form. Yet despite the seeming uniformity of language of individual items, there is variation in the format, printing style, punctuation, and sometimes wording of these wall writings.

Unlike graffiti, which are written directly on a wall (and typically consist of a single line), the materials presented here are copies reproduced and then tacked or taped to walls. They are also much longer than most graffiti. It is curious that many books and articles devoted to graffiti have been published, but almost none on the equally rich tradition of office copier folklore on walls.

45. When You're up to
Your Ass in Alligators . . .

An extremely popular folk notice found in offices across the United States contrasts the ideal world with the real world, or rather the theory with the practice of working in an office. The following version was collected in the accounting office of the University of California, Berkeley, in 1971. (For other versions, see UFFC-PC, 8, YD, 66, and YWIW, [27].)

Notice

The objective of all dedicated company employees should be to thoroughly analyze all situations, anticipate all problems prior to their occurrence, have answers for these problems, and move swiftly to solve these problems when called upon. . . . .
                    However . . . .
when you are up to your ass in alligators, it is difficult to remind yourself that your initial objective was to drain the swamp.

46. Memo to All Personnel

Disputes between union and management are a fact of life in the commercial world. They often affect the life of all citizens, especially when critical services are disrupted. Occasionally, a union may become involved in a jurisdictional controversy with another union, for example, over who shall represent a group of workers. Such interunion struggles may be as bitter as the more usual confrontations between labor and management. The following notice, collected at a General Dynamics office in southern California in 1976, comments on such struggles from the point of view of management.

MEMO

TO   ALL PERSONNEL

FROM   HEADQUARTERS

Due to the fact that the two unions

involved have been unable to agree

upon who shall blow the trumpets,

the end of the world has been

postponed for another two weeks.

GOD   G:pn

When You're up to Your Ass in Alligators . . .

47. A Wise Old Owl

The following item is at least one hundred years old. It is often used to teach children the value of listening rather than speaking. The rhyme is included by Iona and Peter Opie in their *Oxford Dictionary of Nursery Rhymes*. They believe the rhyme to be old but they could not cite any version found before World War I. The fourteenth edition of Bartlett's *Familiar Quotations* cites a full text from *Punch* 68 (1875), 155. The Opies indicate that the rhyme was quoted by John D. Rockefeller in September 1915 and that Calvin Coolidge had the words inscribed over his fireplace. They also note that it appeared on a security placard in France ("Soldiers should imitate that old bird"). See Iona and Peter Opie, *The Oxford Dictionary of Nursery Rhymes* (Oxford: Oxford University Press, 1951), pp. 340–41, no. 394.

The version presented here was collected from a bulletin board in a Naval Reserve Intelligence Office at Andrews Air Force Base in Washington, D.C., in 1975. Evidently, the admonition is still considered relevant to persons working with classified information.

A wise old owl lived in an oak
The more he saw the less he spoke
The less he spoke, the more he heard
Why can't we be like that wise old bird?

48. Deteriorata

A philosophical guide for living called "Desiderata" was copyrighted in 1927 by Max Ehrmann, but it has circulated for many years without any indication of authorship. The guide begins "Go placidly amid the noise and the haste, and remember what peace there may be in silence." It ends "With all its sham, drudgery and broken dreams, it is still a beautiful world. Be cheerful. Strive to be happy." In between is an extended set of inspirational if somewhat sugarcoated pieces of good counsel. (For a recent reprinting of the poem, see Max Ehrmann, *The Desiderata of Happiness* [Boulder, Colorado: Blue Mountain Arts, 1975], pp. 10–11.)

The folk have composed a parody of "Desiderata," which makes fun of the saccharine optimism and wisdom of the original. The version presented here was collected in 1974 at the Naval Air Station in Alameda, California.

DETERIORATA

Go placidly amid the noise and waste, and remember what conflict there may be in owning a piece thereof. Avoid quiet and passive people unless you are in need of sleep. Rotate your tires. Speak glowingly of those greater than yourself and heed well their advice even though they may be turkeys; know what to kiss and when. Consider that two wrongs never make a right, but three do. Whenever possible put people on hold. Be comforted that in the face of aridity and disillusionment and despite the changing fortunes of time, there is always a big fortune in computer maintenance. Remember the Pueblo. Strive at all times to bend, fold, staple, and mutilate. Know yourself; if you need help call the FBI. Exercise caution in your daily affairs, especially with those persons closest to you. That lemon on your left for instance. Be assured that a walk through the ocean of most souls would scarcely get your feet wet. Fall not in love, therefore; it will stick to your face. Gracefully surrender the things of youth, birds, clean air, tuna, Taiwan; and let not the sands of time get in your lunch. Hire people with books. For a good time call 606-4311: ask for Ken. Take heart amid the deepening gloom that your dog is finally getting enough cheese; and reflect whatever misfortune may be your lot, it could only be worse in Milwaukee. You are a fluke of the Universe; you have no right to be here, and whether or not you can hear it, the Universe is laughing behind your back. Therefore, make peace with your God whatever you conceive him to be, Hairy Thunderer or Cosmic Muffin. With all its hopes, dreams, promises, and urban renewal, the world continues to deteriorate.
Give up.

49. We the Willing

The following widely known motto incorporates elements of both boasting and complaining. We present two versions to show the range of variation. Both versions were collected in California in 1975–76. (For four additional versions, see UFFC-TB, 2–5. For another, see YD, 110. For English versions, see YWIW, [121] and TCB, 11 and 77.)

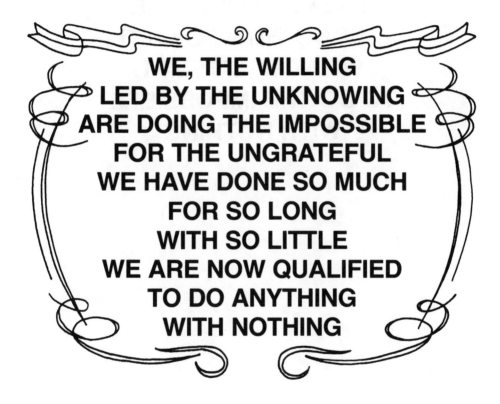

WE, THE WILLING
LED BY THE UNKNOWING
ARE DOING THE IMPOSSIBLE
FOR THE UNGRATEFUL
WE HAVE DONE SO MUCH
FOR SO LONG
WITH SO LITTLE
WE ARE NOW QUALIFIED
TO DO ANYTHING
WITH NOTHING

WE THE UNWILLING
LED BY THE UNQUALIFIED
HAVE BEEN DOING
THE UNBELIEVABLE
SO LONG WITH SO LITTLE
WE NOW ATTEMPT
TO DO THE IMPOSSIBLE
WITH NOTHING

When You're up to Your Ass in Alligators . . .

50. Yea, Though I Walk through the Valley

The Twenty-third Psalm is a favorite for parodists. The fourth verse has been singled out for special treatment in the following widely distributed wall notice. Typically there is a tough-looking cartoon character associated with the verse. The following version was collected in Berkeley in 1971. (For another version, see YD, 70.)

Yea, though I walk through the valley of the shadow of death I shall fear no evil, Cause I am the meanest "Son of a Bitch" in the valley.

The entire Twenty-third Psalm has been used for many years to satirize the federal government in general and the president in particular. Every president since Franklin D. Roosevelt has been honored by being mentioned in this parody and one would guess that future presidents will be similarly treated. The following two versions are representative. The first was collected in Virginia in 1939; the second in San Francisco in 1974. (For four other versions of the presidential psalm, see UFFC-TB, 130–33.)

PARODY

The Government is my shepherd; I need not work. It allows me to lie down on good jobs; it leadeth me beside still factories. It destroyeth my initiative; it leadeth me in the paths of the parasite for politics' sake. Yea, though I walk through the valley of laziness and deficit spending I will fear no evil; for the Government is with me; its doles and its vote-getters, they comfort me. It prepareth an economic Utopia for me by appropriating the earnings of my grandchildren. It filleth my head with bologna; my inefficiency runneth over. Surely, the Government shall care for me all the days of my life, and I shall dwell in a fool's paradise forever.

FORD PSALM

Gerry is my Shepherd, I am in want
he maketh me to lie down on park benches
he leadeth me beside still factories
he restoreth my doubt in the Republican
  party
he leadeth me in the path of
  unemployment for his party's sake
Yea, though I walk through the Valley of
  Soup Kitchens,
I am hungry
he anoynteth my income with taxes
my expenses runneth over my income
surely poverty and hard living will
  follow me
all the days of the Republican
  administration
I shall dwell in a rented house forever

Some versions include the "promised land" sequence previously discussed in UF, 10–11. Other versions, referring to President Nixon, collected in California and Wyoming, included the following traditional postscript. (For another version, see Michael

J. Preston, "Xerox-Lore," *Keystone Folklore* 19 [1974]: 25.)

> I'm glad I'm an American
> I'm glad that I am free
> But I wish I were a doggie
> and Nixon were a tree

51. If the Meek Shall Inherit the Earth

The eternal problem of trying to reconcile aggressive behavior with a pacifist philosophy is not easily solved. The Bible itself is of two minds as George Bernard Shaw devastatingly pointed out in his modern parable *The Adventures of the Black Girl in Her Search for God* published in 1932. The God of the Old Testament is a deity of violence who delights in smiting the enemies of Israel; the God of the New Testament is a deity of love, a champion of peace who advocates turning one's cheek in the face of violence. War and peace are cheek by jowl in the Bible and in life. Perhaps it is a matter of ideal and real. Peace is surely the ideal, but war is too often the reality.

The dilemma is beautifully articulated in the folk's adaptation of the prophecy in Matt. 5:5 (cf. Ps. 37:11) "Blessed are the meek: for they shall inherit the earth." This folk adaptation was collected in Oakland in 1976. (For another version in which the tiger is manning a business office telephone, see UFFC-PC, 100.) A second version, which reportedly circulated in Tennessee in the early 1960s, has a different caption but a similar disconsolate tiger. This Tennessee version is said to be popular among women's liberation groups, perhaps because of the suggestion of male impotence. (For an English variant, see YWIW, [52].)

IF THE MEEK SHALL INHERIT THE EARTH, WHAT THE HELL WILL HAPPEN TO ALL US TIGERS?

When You're up to Your Ass in Alligators . . .

EVERY MAN A TIGER

52. Why Worry?

This exercise in binary reasoning goes back to the early 1950s if not before. Although it is ostensibly designed to minimize worrying, it enumerates some of the things people worry about, such as health and the afterlife. The following version from ISR was collected from the Orange County jail in southern California in 1954. The item enjoyed wide circulation in San Francisco in the early 1970s.

WHY WORRY?

There are only two things to worry about
Either you are well or you are sick.
If you are well there is nothing to worry
  about.
If you are sick there are two things to
  worry about.
Either you will get well or you will die.
If you get well there is nothing to worry
  about.
If you die there are only two things to
  worry about.
Either you go to Heaven or to Hell.
If you go to Heaven there is nothing to
  worry about.
But if you go to Hell you will be so darn
  busy shaking hands with your friends.
You won't have time to worry.

Similar in style is the junior high school item "Why?" or "Why Study?" A version from Los Angeles dating from 1966 is as follows:

WHY?

The more you study
The more you know
The more you know
The more you can forget
The more you can forget
The more you do forget
The more you forget
The less you know
So WHY STUDY!!?

When You're up to Your Ass in Alligators . . .

53. Getting Things Done around Here

Business efficiency is once again depicted in sexual terms. This item was collected in an Oakland department store in 1974. (For other versions, see UFFC-PC, 132, and YD, 8. For a version from England, see YWIW, [73].)

GETTING THINGS DONE

AROUND HERE

IS LIKE MATING ELEPHANTS:

1. It's done at a high level.

2. It's accomplished with a lot of roaring and screaming.

3. AND it takes two years to get any results!!!!!!!

54. If You Can't Dazzle Them

The following folk advice is presented to those with limited mental resources. It was collected in Oakland in 1974. (For another version, see YD, 28.)

If you can't
dazzle them
with brilliance

Baffle them
with bullshit

When You're up to Your Ass in Alligators . . .

55. I Know You Believe You Understand

The consequence of taking the advice of item 54 leads to misunderstandings of the sort described in the following rhetorical contortion. Half of our versions have "I know *that* you believe . . ." and the other half have "I know you believe. . . ." The version below was collected in Salt Lake City in 1971. (For an English text, see YWIW, [39].)

I KNOW THAT YOU BELIEVE YOU UNDERSTAND WHAT YOU THINK I SAID, BUT I AM NOT SURE YOU REALIZE THAT WHAT YOU HEARD IS NOT WHAT I MEANT.

56. The Boss Is Always Right

If an employee thinks the boss is unclear or wrong, the following rules should be kept in mind. The version comes from the Audio-Visual Department of the University of California, San Diego, in 1976. A second version kindly supplied by Gershon Legman indicates a comparable tradition in Cannes, France, in 1975. (For a German version, see IK, 68; for an English version, see TCB, 39.)

Rule No. 1
THE BOSS IS ALWAYS RIGHT!

Rule No. 2
IF THE BOSS IS WRONG, SEE RULE NO. 1

REGLEMENT INTERIEUR

Pour la bonne marche du service

ARTICLE 1 — Le chef a raison.
ARTICLE 2 — Le chef a toujours raison.
ARTICLE 3 — Même si un subalterne a raison c'est l'article 1 qui s'applique.
ARTICLE 4 — Le chef ne mange pas, il se nourrit.
ARTICLE 5 — Le chef ne boit pas, il goûte.
ARTICLE 6 — Le chef ne dort pas, il se repose.
ARTICLE 7 — Le chef n'est pas en retard, il est retenu.
ARTICLE 8 — le chef ne quitte jamais son service, il est appelé.
ARTICLE 9 — Le chef ne lit jamais son journal pendant le service, il l'étudie.
ARTICLE 10 — Le chef n'entretient pas de relations avec sa secrétaire, il l'éduque.
ARTICLE 11 — On entre dans le bureau du chef avec des idées personnelles, on en ressort avec les idées du chef.
ARTICLE 12 — Le chef reste chef, même en caleçon de bain.
ARTICLE 13 — Le chef est obligé de penser pour tout le monde.
ARTICLE 14 — Plus on critique le chef, moins on a de primes.

57. Don't Wait for the Shrimp Boats

One problem with promiscuity aside from the moral issue is the risk of contracting venereal disease or becoming infested with body lice in the genital area. Such lice are commonly referred to as crabs, the subject of the following double entendre collected in Long Beach in 1975 but known to have circulated in Downey, California, about 1960. The caption may represent a triple entendre. In crew parlance, a rower whose oar jams under water is said to have caught a crab. (It is as if a crab had grasped the oar and held it down under the water.) Because the cartoon figure is shown rowing, it is likely that this additional meaning of "crab" is intended. A version known to the authors from oral tradition in the 1950s in Nevada is "Don't wait up for the shrimp boats, Mama, Daddy's coming home with the crabs."

Don't wait for
  the shrimpboats.

I'm coming home.
 with the crabs.

58. No Problem Is So Big

The folk not only offer serious advice about facing individual responsibility, but also make fun of such advice. The following folk adaptation of the Charles Schulz *Peanuts* character Linus was collected from an office wall at the Naval Air Station in Alameda, California, in 1975.

59. A Neat Desk

Some amount of disorder is understood to be a precondition for or consequence of productive work. But not all disorder is productive. Modern psychiatry has suggested that individuals project their personalities into their working and living habits. Thus the following piece of folk psychiatry may not be entirely facetious. A compulsively neat or clean individual may be neurotic. (So also may a compulsively disorderly or dirty person. *Compulsive* is the key word.) The following version was collected in a California office of Container Corporation in 1976. (For an English version, see TCB, 63.)

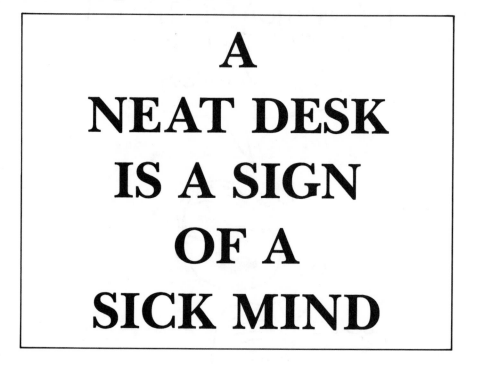

A NEAT DESK IS A SIGN OF A SICK MIND

When You're up to Your Ass in Alligators . . .

60. Thimk, Plan Ahead, and Acurracy

The following folk admonitions illustrate the mistakes warned against. The first two also reflect the future orientation of Americans insofar as Americans are more concerned with thinking ahead than looking back. These two extremely common office signs were collected in Salt Lake City in 1970. The third was collected in the University of California Lockshop in 1978. (For an English version of the second text, see TCB, 57. For variants of all three, see YD, 72.)

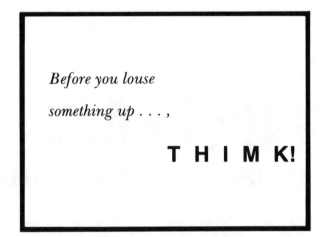

Before you louse

something up . . . ,

T H I M K!

ACURRACY

IS OUR WATCH-WORD

WE NEVER MAKE

MISTEAKS!

61. Attaboy Certificate

Many employers recognize that employees are likely to perform better if there are formal awards for superior service. Such awards are seldom substitute for salary increases or bonuses, but they may improve general employee morale. "Attaboy" is a slang phrase indicating approval, a phrase, according to the *Dictionary of American Slang,* in use since 1910. The certificate presented here suggests that one bit of criticism negates a thousand instances of praiseworthy behavior. From several versions collected in California and Washington, D.C., we have selected the following one from the Audio-Visual Department of the University of California, San Diego, in 1976. (For two other versions, see UFFC-TB, 100–101. For another, see YD, 127.) We have also included one example of an "Awshit" award, collected in Tennessee in 1977, an award specifically referred to in the "Attaboy" certificate. (For an English version, see TCB, 75.)

CERTIFICATE

FOR YOUR VERY OUTSTANDING
PERFORMANCE
YOU ARE AWARDED

ONE ATTABOY

ONE THOUSAND (1,000) "ATTABOYS" qualifies you to be a
LEADER OF MEN, WORK OVERTIME with a SMILE, EXPLAIN
assorted problems to MANAGEMENT, and be looked upon as
a LOCAL HERO, WITHOUT a RAISE in PAY.

CAUTION: ONE (1) "AWSHIT" WIPES THE BOARD CLEAN
AND YOU HAVE TO START OVER AGAIN

TO: _____

FOR YOUR VERY UNBELIEVABLE GOOF, ABSOLUTE DERELICTION OF DUTY, MONUMENTAL BLUNDER, BREACH OF GOOD MANNERS, BRINGING OF THE WRONG ROCK, ETC., YOU ARE AWARDED ---------------

PLEASE HAND IN ALL *ATTABOYS*. YOU WILL BE GOSSIPED ABOUT IN RESTROOMS, SNIGGERED AT BEHIND YOUR BACK, AND HELD IN GENERAL DERISION.

When You're up to Your Ass in Alligators . . .

62. Raffle for a Dog

A popular fund-raising technique in the United States is the raffle; participants purchase tickets, which constitute chances to win a prize. There is a drawing of the tickets and the holders of the winning tickets are awarded the prizes. The following traditional raffle ticket parody comments in verse on the poor quality of some of the merchandise offered at raffles. The version presented here was collected in Clairton, Pennsylvania, in 1976. The ISR collection has almost identical versions from Chicago in 1961 and from Washington, D.C., in 1947.

NO. 2853

Name

Address

RAFFLE FOR A DOG

Nice brown dog, with a big red thing; will be 10 years old if he lives 'till spring. He has four white legs and a hole in his ass. He will piss on your carpet and shit on your grass. His eyes bulge out and his ass sucks wind—he's a damn good dog for the shape he's in.

Give the dog a good home   Take a chance

DONATION — 25¢ PER BOOK

63. Parking Violation

Two of the minor anxieties of motorists are (1) finding a parking place (see item 19) and (2) receiving a parking ticket. Sometimes one is tempted to park illegally but this may result in a ticket and payment of a fine. In the following parody of a parking ticket, the frustration of a driver angry about the sloppy parking of another motorist is vented through humor. Some versions of this extremely common item are entitled "Citizen's Parking Violation" presumably on the analogy of citizen's arrest (a citizen can under specific statutorily prescribed restrictions arrest someone committing a crime). The following version was collected in

California in 1976 (although the use of the term "expressway" rather than "freeway" suggests east coast provenience). (For two other versions, see UFFC-TB, 97–98. For an English version, see YWIW, [80]. For a German variant, see IK, 112.)

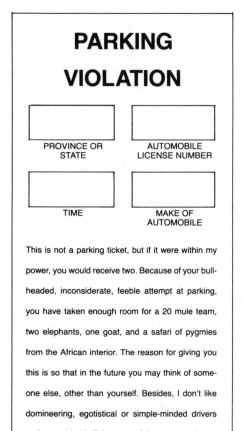

When You're up to Your Ass in Alligators . . .

64. Baggage Ticket

Still another type of ticket is the one used to identify personal possessions being shipped by ship, rail, or air. In this parody from the ISR folklore file, collected from Chicago in 1959, the ostensible goal is to help a drunk get safely home.

I'M OUT ON A H---- OF A TIME!
When I can't stand, tie this to my buttonhole, steal my pocketbook, wind my watch, sponge my clothes.

KickMy AND SHIP ME HOME

My name is _____

Residence _____

Here's How:
Instructions and Tests

Everywhere one goes, one finds rules, instructions, and standard operating procedures to be learned and followed. Complex processes from assembling a tricycle to running a computer are reduced in written form to a series of supposedly simple, foolproof, step-by-step instructions. These instructions have been designed to minimize error and maximize efficiency. However, whatever the merits of such instructions, they are often hard to understand, and their unpleasant authoritarian omniscience encourages individuals to do things their own way—sometimes without even reading all the instructions. Bureaucracy's need for organization, conformity, and controlled behavior conflicts with the individual's need for personal expression and identity.

As Americans are instructed so also are they tested. Often one cannot ignore the world of instructions for fear of the test based on those instructions. At nearly every turn, there are tests to be passed: for driving, physical fitness, professional advancement, educational achievement, and so forth. The individual has little to say about the content of tests. They are designed and administered by authoritarian figures of the kind who issue instructions. Besides required tests, there are some tests taken for fun, such as games, riddles, and puzzles.

The folk instructions and tests presented here are an integral part of the paperwork empire. They provide an unusual reflection of many dominant concerns of modern American society.

65. Compendium of Ground Rules for Laboratory Workers

Perhaps the best known rule for scientists and technicians is Murphy's Law, the most famous example of which is "If anything can go wrong, it will." (For a discussion of Murphy's Laws, see UF, 69–75. For a popular listing of the laws, see Arthur Bloch, *Murphy's Law and Other Reasons Why Things Go Wrong* [Los Angeles: Price, Stern, Sloan, 1977] and Jim Russell, *Murphy's Law* [Millbrae, California: Celestial Arts, 1978].) There are many corollaries of Murphy's Law. For example: "The bread always falls buttered-side down." "A misplaced object always turns up in the last place you look for it." The following list of ground rules collected from the Physiology Department of the University of California, Berkeley, in 1967, illustrates the genre. (For a much longer version, see UFFC-TB, 84.) A version collected in Tennessee in 1977 is entitled "Rules for Experimenters" and it contains such advice as "Publish first, then confirm the experiment" and "Never repeat a successful experiment."

Compendium of Ground Rules for Laboratory Workers

1. *When you don't know what you're doing, do it neatly.*
2. *First draw your curves, then plot the data.*
3. *Experience is directly proportional to the equipment ruined.*
4. *Experiments must be reproducible. They should all fail the same way.*
5. *A record of data is essential. It indicates you have been working.*
6. *In case of doubt, make it sound positive and convincing.*
7. *Do not believe in miracles, depend on them.*
8. *Teamwork is essential in the lab. It allows you to blame someone else.*

When You're up to Your Ass in Alligators . . .

66. Itemized Bill

The value of expertise is sometimes difficult to assess in dollars. What determines how much a surgeon, trial lawyer, or any professional specialist charges for his services? Sometimes the ease with which an expert performs a complex task is deceptive. Yet it is precisely the apparent ease that is often the mark of the true expert. The following anecdote about an invoice for services rendered occurs in oral tradition and in copier form. The version was collected in Woodland, California, in 1967. (For another version, see Sanford Triverton, *Complete Book of Ethnic Jokes* [New York: Galahad Books, 1981], p. 30.)

ITEMIZED BILL

Shortly before his death in 1923, Charles Steinmetz, the electrical genius, was asked by Henry Ford to help solve a problem that was troubling Ford engineers. A huge generator at the River Rouge Plant was performing poorly. When Steinmetz arrived at the plant, he turned down all assistance, asking only for a notebook, pencil, and cot. For two days and nights he listened to the generator and made numerous computations. Then he asked for a ladder, a measuring tape, and chalk. He climbed the ladder, made careful measurements, and put a chalk mark on the side of the generator. He told his skeptical audience to remove a plate from the side of the generator and take out 16 windings from the field coil at that location. The generator worked perfectly from then on. Subsequently Ford received a bill for $10,000 signed by Steinmetz for GE. Ford returned the bill, acknowledging the good job by Steinmetz but respectfully requesting an itemized statement. Replied Steinmetz:

Making chalk mark on generator .... $	1
Knowing where to make mark.......................	9,999
Total due	$10,000

67. How to Write Good

The title of this item demonstrates the central organizing principle of this listing of rules for writers. The principle consists of illustrating an error of grammar or punctuation in the very sentences warning against such errors. The same technique has been employed in other folk catalogs of grammatical do's and don't's. See "Grammar as Wrote" in UF, 38, and "Report Writing" in TCB, 46. This version was collected in Kokomo, Indiana, in 1968.

HOW TO WRITE GOOD

Subject and verb always has to agree.

Being bad grammar, the writer will not use dangling participles.

Prepositions should not be used to end sentences with.

Parallel construction with coordinate conjunctions is not only an aid to clarity but also is the mark of a good writer.

Do not use a foreign term when there is an adequate English *quid pro quo.*

If you must use a foreign term, it is *de rigor* to use it correctly.

It behooves the writer to avoid archaic expressions.

Do not use hyperbole; not one writer in a million can use it effectively.

Avoid clichés like the plague.

Mixed metaphors are a pain in the neck and ought to be thrown out the window.

In scholarly writing, don't use contractions.

A truly good writer is always especially careful to practically eliminate the too-frequent use of adverbs.

Use a comma before nonrestrictive clauses which are a common source of difficulty.

Placing a comma between subject and predicate, is not correct.

Parenthetical words however should be enclosed in commas.

Consult the dictionary frequently to avoid mispelling.

68. First Aid Howlers

One can learn from mistakes. The following item collected in Paducah, Kentucky, in 1976 is similar in style to "Automobile Accident Insurance Claims" (see item 36).

FIRST AID HOWLERS

People don't always do as they say and sometimes it's a good thing they don't.

Take for example, answers given by some fourth-graders in a first aid test. Following these instructions would result in some pretty unusual situations. The prescribed treatments were as follows:

FOR HEAD COLDS: "Use an agonizer to spray the nose until it drops in the throat."

FOR NOSE BLEEDS: "Put the nose lower than the body."

FOR SNAKE BITE: "Bleed the wound and rape the victim in a blanket for shock."

FOR FRACTURES: "To see if the limb is broken, wiggle it gently back and forth."

FOR FAINTING: "Rub the person's chest, or if it's a lady, rub her arm above the hand."

FOR ASPHYXIA-TION: "Apply artificial respiration until the victim is dead."

69. The Art of Communication

A party game often used as an instructional technique in elementary school to show the fallibility of human communication consists of someone whispering a sentence to the person next to him. This person whispers in turn to the next person. The last person to receive the whispered message says it aloud, and this version, usually garbled, is then compared with the original. The game shows in miniature how distortion and error can creep into texts transmitted from one person to another. For a discussion of experimental attempts to replicate this folkloristic phenomenon, see F. C. Bartlett, "Some Experiments on the Reproduction of Folk Stories" in Alan Dundes, ed., *The Study of Folklore* (Englewood Cliffs: Prentice-Hall, 1965), pp. 243–58. In the following text collected from a naval reserve commander in Jamaica Estates, New York, in 1971, the fate of an order as it passes down the chain of command is detailed.

The Art of Communication

The Captain issued the following order to his executive officer: "Tomorrow evening at approximately 2000, Halley's comet will be visible in the northern sky, an event which occurs only once every 75 years. Have the men fall out on the flight deck in undress blues, and I shall explain this rare phenomenon to them. In case of rain, we shall not be able to see anything so assemble the men on the hanger bay and I shall show them films of it."

Clear enough. So the exec wrote to the operations officer.

"By order of the captain, tomorrow evening at 2000, Halley's comet will appear on the flight deck. If it rains, fall the men out in undress blues, then march them to the hanger bay where this rare phenomenon will take place, something which occurs once every 75 years."

The ops officer thereupon instructed his first lieutenant:

"By order of the captain in undress blues at 2000 tomorrow evening, the phenomenal Halley's comet will appear in the theatre. In case of rain on the flight deck, the captain will give another order, something which occurs every 75 years."

Snapped the first lieutenant to his chief: "Tomorrow at 2000, the Captain will appear in the theatre with Halley's comet, something which happens every 75 years. If it rains, the Captain will order the comet onto the flight deck."

And the chief told his men: "When it rains tomorrow at 2000 the phenomenal 75-year old Admiral Halley, accompanied by the Captain, will fly his comet onto the flight deck into the hanger bay area in undress blues."

When You're up to Your Ass in Alligators . . .

70. The Halloween Party

How (not) to put one over on your spouse is the subject of an elaborate catch, collected coast to coast. This joke depends on the old-fashioned dramatic devices of disguise and concealed identity. Halloween is a festival at which ritual reversals are permitted—little boys can dress up as little girls, girls can dress up as boys, children can dress as adults and can enter the homes of strangers, and so forth. For this reason, the Halloween party setting provides a suitable frame for the reversal that is the basis of this story. The text was collected in Concord, New Hampshire, in 1977. Other versions (not presented here) dating from the early 1960s are almost identical. (For an additional text, see UFFC-TB, 144. For an English text, see TCB, 147.)

A couple was invited to a real swanky Halloween party, so the wife got costumes for both of them. On the night of the party she developed a terrible headache and told her husband to go without her. He protested, but she said that all she was going to do was take a couple of aspirin and go to bed and there was no need of his good time being spoiled by not attending. So he got into his costume and off he went. The wife, after sleeping soundly for about an hour, awoke without a sign of pain and as it was just a little after nine, she decided to go to the party. Inasmuch as her husband did not know what kind of costume she was to wear, she thought it would be a good idea to just slip into the party and observe how he acted when she was not around.

This she did and as soon as she joined the party, the first one she spied was her husband cavorting around the dance floor, dancing with first one slick chick and then another—copping a little feel here and there. So the wife sidled up to him, and being a rather seductive babe herself, he left his partner standing high and dry and devoted his attention to the new stuff that had just arrived.

She let him go as far as he wished, naturally, and finally he whispered a little proposition in her ear. This she agreed to and they went out to one of the cars parked nearby—etc.—etc.—etc.—? Just before the unmasking at midnight, she slipped away, and went home and got into bed, wondering what kind of explanation her husband would make as to his behavior. He arrived home about 1:30 A.M. and came right into the bedroom to see how she was. She was sitting up in bed reading and asked, "What kind of time did you have?" He said, "Oh, the same old stuff. You know I never have a good time when you aren't around." Then she asked, "Did you dance much?" and he said, "Well, I'll tell you. I never danced once. When I got there, Peter Jones, Bill Brown and some other guys were stag too, so we went back into the den and played poker the rest of the evening, but I'll tell you one thing. That fellow I loaned my costume to sure had one hell of a good time."

71. Regulation on the Sale of Cabbages

Of the approximately five hundred items of office copier folklore we have collected, the only one to our knowledge to have been studied in depth is a curious statistical concatenation concerned with cabbages. Yet Max Hall in his interesting essay "The Great Cabbage Hoax: A Case Study" fails to realize that he is dealing with folklore. Instead, he describes the item as a hoax or deliberate deception, which he claims he has spent nearly thirty years trying to expose and disprove.

Hall says he first heard the item on August 9, 1951—although he also states that it had circulated earlier in the 1940s during World War II. He proceeds to track the item through a maze of ephemeral house organs, bulletins, news stories, and radio quiz programs. However, he seems puzzled at the remarkable vitality of the item as it continues in tradition. Of course, because the subject is the amount of government regulation on the conduct of business, and because the number of government regulations has proliferated astronomically, it is no wonder that the item has continued to find favor with anyone who has run afoul of a government regulation or ordinance.

The central premise of the item is that there is an inverse relationship between the significance of a subject and the number of words employed to describe that subject. The less important the subject, the greater the number of words devoted to it. The item came into the public eye in 1977 when it was discussed at some length in the *New Republic*.

The *New Republic* editors tried to find the source of the item, which they had first noticed in a Mobil Oil advertisement in the

New York Times Magazine for April 10, 1977. They telephoned the New York public affairs office of Mobil only to discover that the item had been borrowed from the fall 1976 edition of *Progress*, the house organ of FMC (formerly Food Machinery Corporation) in Chicago. A call to FMC revealed that they had borrowed the item from the May 5, 1976, edition of NAM *Reports*, the organ of the National Association of Manufacturers headquartered in Washington, D.C. When questioned, the editor of the NAM publication stated that she had obtained it from an NAM director whose name she could not remember, "who had it printed on a card he carried around with him."

The *New Republic* essay concluded with respect to government control of cabbages: "There is no such regulation and there never was. By some miracle, the federal government apparently does not specifically regulate the sale of cabbages at all." However, a reader was quick to respond that there are indeed "United States Standards for Cabbage" set forth in the *Code of Federal Regulations*, standards that run to approximately fifteen hundred words.

None of those who have previously written about the cabbage regulation have recognized that the item is folkloristic. The factual historicity of the item or the lack thereof is not nearly so important as the reasons why this item has continued to be meaningful to much of the American public. For the above-mentioned discussions, see Max Hall, "The Great Cabbage Hoax: A Case Study," *Journal of Personality and Social Psychology* 2 (1965): 563–69. See also "26,911 Little Words," *New Republic* 176, no. 17 (April 23, 1977), pp. 9–10; and Robert P. Kemmy, "Last Word on Cabbages," *New Republic* 176, no. 20 (May 14, 1977), p. 7.

We present here the Mobil Oil text:

> The Lord's Prayer has 56 words; at Gettysburg, Lincoln spoke only 268 long-remembered words; and we got a whole country goin' on the 1,322 words in the Declaration of Independence. So how come it took the federal government 26,911 words to issue a regulation on the sale of cabbages?

72. How You Can Tell When It's Going to Be a Rotten Day

Another traditional set of rules or signs purports to signal the beginning of a day of bad luck. The following version collected in Austin, Texas, in 1980 contains a number of allusions that may not necessarily be well understood in decades to come. For example, one needs to know that "60 Minutes" is a popular television program specializing in investigative reporting of alleged scandals and criminal behavior and that singer Anita Bryant waged a one-woman campaign against homosexuality to fully appreciate all the nuances of the bad-day signs. (For another version, see YD, 42.)

How You Can Tell When it's Going To Be
A Rotten Day

You wake up face down on the pavement.

You put your bra on backward and it fits better.

You call Suicide Prevention and they put you on hold.

You see a "60 Minutes" news team waiting in your office.

Your birthday cake collapses from the weight of the candles.

Your son tells you he wishes Anita Bryant would mind her own business.

You want to put on the clothes you wore home from the party and there aren't any.

You turn on the news and they're showing emergency routes out of the city.

Your twin sister forgot your birthday.

You wake up and discover your waterbed broke and then realize that you don't have a waterbed.

Your car horn goes off accidentally and remains stuck as you follow a group of Hell's Angels on the freeway.

Your wife wakes up feeling amorous and you have a headache.

Your boss tells you not to bother to take off your coat.

The bird singing outside your window is a buzzard.

You wake up and your braces are locked together.

You walk to work and find your dress is stuck in the back of your pantyhose.

You call your answering service and they tell you it's none of your business.

Your blind date turns out to be your ex-wife.

Your income tax check bounces.

You put both contact lenses in the same eye.

Your pet rock snaps at you.

Your wife says, "Good morning, Bill" and your name is George.

Author Unknown . . . But Troubled.

73. Life after Forty

Another set of signs details some of the problems associated with aging. Modern medicine has increased the average life span so that there are ever-increasing numbers of persons concerned with how to cope with the prospect of the infirmities accompanying old age. The humor masks genuine anxiety. The following text was collected in Pittsburg, Texas, in January 1983. (For another version, see YD, 144. For an extended discussion of the significance of the number "forty," see Stanley Brandes, *Forty: The Age and the Symbol* [Knoxville: University of Tennessee Press, 1985].)

LIFE AFTER 40
HOW TO KNOW YOU'RE GROWING OLDER . . .

EVERYTHING HURTS AND WHAT DOESN'T HURT DOESN'T WORK.

THE GLEAM IN YOUR EYES IS FROM THE SUN HITTING YOUR BIFOCALS.

YOU FEEL LIKE THE NIGHT BEFORE AND YOU HAVEN'T BEEN ANYWHERE.

YOUR LITTLE BLACK BOOK CONTAINS ONLY NAMES ENDING IN M.D.

YOU GET WINDED PLAYING CHESS.

YOUR CHILDREN BEGIN TO LOOK MIDDLE AGED.

YOU JOIN A HEALTH CLUB AND DON'T GO.

YOU BEGIN TO OUTLIVE ENTHUSIASM.

YOUR MIND MAKES CONTRACTS YOUR BODY CAN'T MEET.

YOU KNOW ALL THE ANSWERS, BUT NOBODY ASKS YOU THE QUESTIONS.

YOU LOOK FORWARD TO A DULL EVENING.

YOUR FAVORITE PART OF THE NEWSPAPER IS "25 YEARS AGO TODAY."

When You're up to Your Ass in Alligators . . .

YOU SIT IN A ROCKING CHAIR AND CAN'T GET IT GOING.

YOUR KNEES BUCKLE AND YOUR BELT WON'T.

YOU REGRET ALL THOSE MISTAKES RESISTING TEMPTATION.

YOU'RE 17 AROUND THE NECK AND 42 AROUND THE WAIST.

YOU STOP LOOKING FORWARD TO YOUR NEXT BIRTHDAY.

DIALING LONG DISTANCE WEARS YOU OUT.

YOUR BACK GOES OUT MORE THAN YOU DO.

A FORTUNE TELLER OFFERS TO READ YOUR FACE.

YOU TURN OUT THE LIGHT FOR ECONOMIC REASONS RATHER THAN ROMANTIC ONES.

YOU REMEMBER TODAY, THAT YESTERDAY WAS YOUR WEDDING ANNIVERSARY.

YOU ARE STARTLED THE FIRST TIME YOU ARE ADDRESSED AS "OLD TIMER."

YOU BURN THE MIDNIGHT OIL AFTER 9:00 P.M.

YOU SINK YOUR TEETH INTO A STEAK AND THEY STAY THERE.

YOUR PACEMAKER MAKES THE GARAGE DOOR GO UP WHEN YOU SEE A PRETTY GIRL WALK BY.

YOU GET YOUR EXERCISE ACTING AS A PALLBEARER FOR YOUR FRIENDS WHO EXERCISE.

YOU GET TOO MUCH ROOM IN THE HOUSE AND NOT ENOUGH ROOM IN THE MEDICINE CABINET.

THE BEST PART OF YOUR DAY IS OVER WHEN YOUR ALARM GOES OFF.

HAVE A GOOD DAY!!!

74. How to Tell Republicans from Democrats

Party behavior can also refer to political groups. The following differentiation between Republicans and Democrats, reportedly published in the Republican Congressional Committee newsletter in 1974, appeared in the *San Francisco Chronicle* (October 10, 1974), p. 13, and in *Time* (October 21, 1974), p. 28. The newspaper version ended with the statement: "The GOP said the author was unknown."

Democrats buy most of the books that have been banned somewhere. Republicans form censorship committees and read them as a group.

Republicans consume three-fourths of all the rutabagas produced in this country. The remainder is thrown out.

Republicans usually wear hats and almost always clean their paint brushes.

Republicans employ exterminators. Democrats step on the bugs.

Democrats eat the fish they catch. Republicans hang them on the wall.

Republican boys date Democratic girls. They plan to marry Republican girls, but feel they're entitled to a little fun first.

Republicans sleep in twin beds—some even in separate rooms. That is why there are more Democrats.

75. The Joke of the Year

Some jokes are transmitted by office copier though of the total number of oral texts in tradition, only a few are reproduced by this means. One joke found in copier form is the following text, collected in Kokomo, Indiana, in 1967, at a J. C. Penney store. Legman (NLM, 837, 867) cites several versions, one of which was collected from a young woman in Los Angeles in 1940.

THE JOKE-OF-THE-YEAR
VOTED FUNNIEST BY 54 PER CENT OF THE MEMBERS
WHO CAST A BALLOT

After attending an afternoon cocktail party where rich foods and exotic drinks were in abundance, a young Miss boarded a crosstown bus and comfortably settled down for the ride home. Soon thereafter she began to experience gas pains which increased in frequency and intensity. Since crosstown bus service was very infrequent, she became quite concerned about her situation. She did not want to leave the bus to seek relief and then have to wait for another one, so she began to devise some way to remain aboard and still overcome her problem.

Observing that the bus stopped at every intersection for a stop sign, and, in the process of stopping and shifting gears to get started, a considerable amount of noise was generated, she decided that this was an ideal situation and that it would provide sufficient disturbance to cover the sound of "relief." To be sure of correct timing, she closely observed the sequence of events at each stop for the next few blocks and, then decided that the next one was it. As the bus came closer all systems were "go" and, at the predetermined instant, the "blast-off" was triggered. Unfortunately, there was no stop at this intersection and no background support. The blast rang loud and clear.

The young lady was very embarrassed at the turn of events. Finally, she felt that striking up a conversation with the gentleman sitting between her and the window might help to relieve the tension. She said to him, "I beg your pardon sir, but did you get a transfer when you boarded the bus?" He replied, "Hell no lady, but as we pass the next tree I'll grab a handful of leaves for you."

76. How's Your Brain?

Often in wallet card form, this item is designed to test the observational powers of an individual. It was collected in Port Chicago, California, about 1958. In a 1974 version from San Francisco, the text begins with "Finished Files" rather than "Federal Fuses." The answer to the question asked is printed on the reverse side of the card.

HOW'S YOUR BRAIN?

READ THIS SENTENCE:

FEDERAL FUSES ARE THE RESULT OF YEARS OF SCIENTIFIC STUDY COMBINED WITH THE EXPERIENCE OF YEARS.

Now count the F's in that sentence. Only once, don't go back and count them again. You will find the answer on the back and it will tell you something about how good your brain is.

There are six F's in the sentence. An average intelligence finds three of them. If you spotted four, you're above average. If you got five, you can turn up your nose at most anybody. If you caught all six, you're a genius, and a lot too good to be wasting your time on foolishness like this.

When You're up to Your Ass in Alligators . . .

77. The Punctuation Test

The object of this and similar tests is to make sense of a series of words by figuring out the correct intonation pattern. In written form, this means determining a reasonable punctuation scheme. A single clue may be given: It is not all one sentence. The text below was collected in Berkeley in 1974.

John where James had had had had had had had had had had had the teacher's approval.

The answer: John, where James had had "had," had had "had had." "Had had" had had the teacher's approval. In other words, on a grammar quiz, John wrote "had had" and James wrote "had." John's answer was correct because "had had" was what the teacher wanted. Had enough? Another example of this form is: "She said that that that that that that student had was wrong." The meaning is: She said that: that that "that," that that student had, was wrong.

78. Spelling Test

If punctuation bedevils writers of all ages, so also does spelling. The following text was collected in San Francisco in 1974.

SPELLING TEST

In the proximity of a cemetery sat a harassed pediatrician and an embarrassed oculist picnicking on a desiccated apple and gazing at the symmetry of a lady's ankle with unparalleled ecstasy.

NOTE: This test is to be administered to prospective secretaries and stenographers. It is to be taken in *shorthand* and transcribed accurately without any misspellings. It contains the most frequently misspelled words in the English language with the possible exception of *misspell!*

79. Do You Know Your Baseball?

The rebus is an ancient form of folklore in which a word or phrase is conveyed by a letter or pictographic representation, for example, a picture of an eye stands for the pronoun *I*. A typical risqué rebus collected in Oakland in 1974 is:

This reads: Holy mackerel sapphire, look at the hare on that pussy! (For another version, see UFFC-TB, 174.)

The following rebus was collected in San Francisco in 1976. The second version was collected in Clairton, Pennsylvania, in 1976. (For another version, see UFFC-PC, 54.)

When You're up to Your Ass in Alligators . . .

DO YOU KNOW YOUR BASEBALL ?

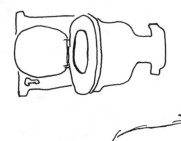

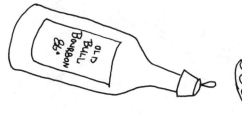

OLD BULL BOURBON 86°

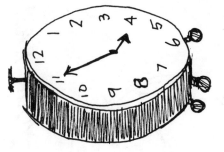

WHAT'S THE SCORE ?

KNOW YOUR BASEBALL? WHAT'S THE SCORE?

For those who may not be familiar with baseball jargon, the message is: Five to four, bottom of the fifth, one out, nobody on. In terms of symbols of American culture, it is interesting that the national pastime is depicted with reference to time and toilet, and breast and bottle.

80. Wordplay

A special form of the rebus plays on the placement of letters or words. For example, a postman is handed a letter addressed as follows:

$$\frac{\text{Wood}}{\text{John}} \qquad \frac{\text{And}}{\text{Mass}}$$

Where and to whom should the postman deliver the letter? Obviously to John Underwood in Andover, Massachusetts. (For a variant consisting of:

Wood
John
Mass

see Jan H. Brunvand, *The Study of American Folklore* [New York, 1968], p. 56.)

Another example of this folkloristic form collected from an English informant who learned it in North Riding, Yorkshire, in 1937, illustrates the technique:

man   B   wife
meddling

The message to be deciphered here is proverbial advice, namely B(e) above "meddling" between "man" and "wife." For an enlightening discussion of this fascinating type of folklore, see Michael J. Preston, "The English Literal Rebus and the Graphic Riddle Tradition," *Western Folklore* 41 (1982): 104–38.

The "Wordplay" text presented here was collected in Danville, California, in 1977 from an informant who obtained it from his secretary who had obtained it from her son who had obtained it from a professor at the University of California, Davis. The text itself contained an indication that it was circulating widely among educators in Oregon. The object is to identify the word or phrase depicted.

Wordplay

1. EZ / iiiii

2. T O U C H

3. MOTH CRY CRY

4. BLACK / COAT

5. TIME TIME

6. S A N D

7. HURRY

8. **AGES**

9. O / M.D. PH.D. L.L.D.

10. MAN / BOARD

11. R|E|A|D|I|N|G

12. WEAR / LONG

13. DICE DICE

14. i i i i O O

15. CYCLE CYCLE CYCLE

16. ECNALG

17. T O W N

18. BUD/GET

19. R ROAD A D

20. LE VEL

21. STAND / I

22. CAKE

23. change

24. MeQUIT

25. S U N

26. HE's|HIMSELF

27. KNEE / LIGHT

28. U P

1. Easy on the eyes

2. Touchdown

3. Mothballs

4. Black overcoat

5. Double time

6. Sand slide

7. Hurry up

8. Dark Ages

9. 3 degrees below zero

10. Man overboard

11. Reading between the lines

12. Long underwear

13. Paradise

14. Circles under the eyes

15. Tricycle

16. Backward glance

17. Downtown

18. Cutting budget in half

19. Crossroads

20. Split level

21. I understand

22. Upside-down cake

23. Small change

24. Quit following me

25. Sunrise

26. He's beside himself

27. Neon light

28. Split up

81. Twelve Hidden Books
of the New Testament

The puzzle genre is also found in a religious context. The following example was collected at a family reunion in Abilene, Texas, in July 1975. The object is to locate the names of twelve of the books of the New Testament that are concealed in the text. The text is sufficiently well constructed so that even a knowledge of the names does not automatically ensure success in finding them

TWELVE HIDDEN BOOKS OF THE NEW TESTAMENT

Jesus was a man whose acts indicated he was a teacher from God. The standard he set provides the mark of excellence in every human life. Jesus' standard is strict. It usually requires drastic changes in one's life.

On one occasion Jesus visited in the home of friends. His host said, "Let Mary prepare you some broth—she brews the best in Judea; and let her fetch you some jam, especially some made from this year's figs." As they gathered around the table the youngest son presented himself for the evening meal. His father said, "Tim, O thy hands are dirty from playing with your pet ermine. Go wash and call John."

After the meal the host called for the players of instruments and asked one of the maids to play upon the four-stringed full uke. The host said to Jesus as the maid played, "While the Romans rule Palestine there is little to sing about. It will be a great revelation when the Messiah comes and breaks the yoke of Roman oppression."

For those whose knowledge of the Bible is limited, the hidden books are: Acts, Mark, Titus, Hebrews, Jude, James, Timothy, Peter, John, Luke, Romans, and Revelation.

When You're up to Your Ass in Alligators . . .

82. Message to Hotel Clerk

The following puzzle, which some may find difficult to solve, revolves around an ingeniously coded exchange between a young female guest at a hotel and the desk clerk. To fully appreciate the puzzle, readers may wish to photocopy this page so that it can be viewed properly. (If copying facilities are not immediately available, the puzzle can be solved by tracing or by copying exactly the "numerical" messages on a piece of plain paper. By holding the reverse side of the paper up to the light, one can distinguish the printed messages.) This version is from ISR. It was collected in Chicago in 1959.

A young lady guest at a prominent hotel telephoned a message to the clerk on duty. The above is her frantic appeal, and the courteous clerk's answer

?

83. How to Control the Birthrate

Another common technique in copier folklore involves hidden communications concealed by pseudoscript from another culture. The following examples give the appearance of being in Chinese, Arabic, and Japanese respectively. The texts make little sense in those languages. A translation of the Arabic text, for example, is roughly "Dates hanging under the fortress of Aleppo." The messages are revealed in English only after the item is folded. The first version was collected in California in 1976, the second is from ISR, and the third, also from ISR, was collected in Washington, D.C., in 1947. Because it is difficult to see the messages without actually folding the items, we present each item before and after folding. (For a German version of the Chinese example, see IK, 28.)

How to Control the Birthrate

by Eminent Chinese Specialist Hu Shin Fu

How to Birthrate

*by E*ecialist

SLEEP ALONE

When You're up to Your Ass in Alligators . . .

ANCIENT ARABIC FORMULA FOR SURE BIRTH
CONTROL.— STILL RECOMMENDED TO-DAY.

NO FUCK

What The Japs Can Do
To Every American

84. Aptitude Test

A test of a different sort makes use of traditional trick questions. It may be a not-so-subtle commentary on the fact that many examinations in school contexts involve trick or tricky questions. Some of the tricks in the following version, collected in San Francisco in 1974, depend on attention to small details. The side of United States coins that bears the denomination, for example, "quarter dollar," does *not* contain the four words "In God We Trust" but rather "United States of America." A dog cannot run more than halfway into the woods before he starts leaving them. Thirty divided by one-half is sixty, not fifteen, and so on. (For another version, see UFFC-TB, 89.)

APTITUDE TEST

1. If you went to bed at 8:00 o'clock at night, and set the alarm to get up at 9:00 in the morning, how many hours sleep would this permit you to have?
2. Do they have a 4th of July in England?
3. How many birthdays does the average man have?
4. Why can't a man living in Winston-Salem, North Carolina, be buried west of the Mississippi?
5. If you had only one match and entered a room in which there was a kerosene lamp, an oil heater, and a wood burning stove, which would you light first?
6. Some months have 30 days and some months have 31 days. How many months have 28 days?
7. If a doctor gave you three pills and told you to take one every ½ hour, how long would they last?
8. A man builds a house with four sides to it and it is rectangular in shape. Each side has a southern exposure. A big bear comes wandering by. What color is the bear?
9. How far can a dog run into the woods?
10. What four words appear on each denomination of a U.S. coin?
11. What is the minimum number of active baseball players on the field during any part of an inning? How many outs in each inning?
12. I have in my hand two (2) U.S. coins which total 55¢ in value. One is not a nickel. (PLEASE BEAR IN MIND THAT ONE IS NOT A NICKEL.) What are the two coins?

13. A farmer has 17 sheep. All of the sheep but 9 died and were buried. How many did he have left?
14. Divide 30 by ½ and add 10. What is the answer?
15. Take two apples from three apples and what do you have?
16. Two men played checkers. They played 5 games and each man won the same number of games. How come?
17. A woman gives a beggar 50¢. The woman is the beggar's sister, but the beggar is not the woman's brother. How come?
18. How many animals of each species did Moses take aboard the ark with him?
19. In North Carolina, can a man marry his widow's sister?
20. An archaeologist claims he found some old coins dated 46 B.C. Do you think he did?
21. What word in this test is mispelled?

85. There Are Five Houses

A much more demanding test, which involves elimination and logical deduction, assumes the existence of five houses each with its own characteristics. The occupants may drive different makes of automobiles or, as in the example below, smoke different brands of cigarettes. Most individuals will require pencil and paper to determine the answers to the two specific questions asked. The following version was collected in San Francisco in 1974. (For an English version, see TCB, 88.)

1. There are five houses, all with a different color and in which there live men of different nationality. They also have different drinking habits, pets and cigarettes.
2. The Englishman lives in the red house.
3. The Spaniard owns the dog.
4. Coffee is the drink in the green house.
5. The Ukrainian drinks tea.
6. The green house is located at the right-hand side of the white house.
7. The "Old Gold" smoker keeps snails.
8. "Kool" is smoked in the yellow house.

9. Milk is the drink in the house in the middle.
10. The Norwegian lives in the first house at the left-hand side.
11. The man who smokes "Chesterfield" lives in the house next to the man with the fox.
12. "Kool" is smoked in the house next to the house where they keep a horse.
13. The "Lucky-Strike" smoker drinks orange juice.
14. The Japanese smokes "Parliament."
15. The Norwegian lives next to the blue house.

QUESTIONS

1. Who drinks water?
2. And who owns the zebra?

The following is the solution to the puzzle:

HOUSES	Yellow	blue	red	ivory
INHABI-TANTS	Norwegian	Ukrainian	Englishman	Spaniard
PETS	fox	horse	snails	dog
BEVERAGES	water	tea	milk	orange juice
CIGARETTES	Kool	Chesterfield	Old Gold	Lucky Strike

HOUSES	green
INHABITANTS	Japanese
PETS	zebra
BEVERAGES	coffee
CIGARETTES	Parliament

Norwegian drinks water. Japanese owns the zebra.

Although the valuable collections of copier materials from Colorado did not include a version of "There Are Five Houses," they do contain an interesting baseball variant employing a similar technique. The text in UFFC-TB, 171, goes as follows:

Nine men, Brown, White, Black, Miller, Green, Gray, Wilson, Jones, and Smith, play on a baseball team.

1. Smith and Brown each won $10 playing poker with the pitcher.
2. Gray was taller than Wilson and shorter than White, but each of them weighed more than the first baseman.
3. The third baseman lives in the same apartment as Jones.
4. Miller and the outfielders play bridge in their spare time.
5. White, Miller, Brown, the right fielder and the center fielder are bachelors, and the rest are married.
6. Wilson and Black, one of them plays an outfield position.
7. The right fielder is shorter than the center fielder.
8. The third baseman is a brother to the pitcher's wife.
9. Green is taller than the infielders and battery (pitcher and catcher), except Jones, Smith, and Black.
10. The second baseman beat Jones, Brown, Gray and the catcher at cards.
11. The third baseman, the shortstop, and Gray made $130 apiece, speculating in U.S. Steel.
12. The second baseman is engaged to Miller's sister.
13. Black hates the catcher, and lives in the same house as his sister.
14. Brown, Black, and the shortstop lost $200 apiece, speculating in copper.
15. The catcher has three daughters, the third baseman has two sons; Green was being sued for divorce.

NAME THE POSITIONS PLAYED BY EACH MAN!!!!!!

The solution, according to UFFC-TB, 174, is as follows: Brown plays first base; White second base; Black third base; Miller shortstop; Green left field; Gray center field; Wilson right field; Jones pitcher; and Smith catcher. It is noted that other solutions may be possible.

86. Situation Adaptability Evaluation for Management Personnel

Psychological tests may be administered to prospective managerial candidates to gauge their suitability for executive positions. The tests typically pose hypothetical problems or situations, which the candidate is asked to solve or explain. The answers are scored and evaluated by psychologists. The following text collected in Tennessee in 1977 parodies these tests. One recurrent theme is the difficulty in indulging in some body functions in a formal setting. This may poke fun at the notion that a good manager is able to keep everything under control. (For an English version containing six of the eight questions on the test, see TCB, 82–83.)

SITUATION ADAPTABILITY EVALUATION

FOR MANAGEMENT PERSONNEL

This test has been designed to evaluate reactions of management personnel to various situations. The situations are based on actual case studies from a well-known educational institution and represent a cross section of test data correlated to evaluate both reaction time to difficult situations as well as the soundness of each decision selected.

There are eight multiple choice questions. Read each question thoroughly. Place an "x" by the answer you feel is most correctly justified by circumstances given. Be prepared to justify your decision.

You have four (4) minutes! (Do not turn this page until told to do so.)

1. You have prepared a proposal for the regional director of purchasing for your largest customer. The success of this presentation will mean increasing your sales to his company by 200%. In the middle of your proposal the customer leans over to look at your report and spits into your coffee. You:

_ a. Tell him you prefer your coffee black.

_ b. Ask to have him checked for any communicable dis-
eases.

_ c. Take a leak in his "out" basket.

2. You are having lunch with a prospective customer talking
   about what could be your biggest sale of the year. During the
   conversation a blonde walks into the restaurant and she is so
   stunning you draw your companion's attention to her and give
   a vivid description of what you would do if you had her alone
   in your motel. She walks over to your table and introduces
   herself as your client's daughter. Your next move is to:

   _ a. Ask for her hand in marriage.

   _ b. Pretend you've forgotten how to speak English.

   _ c. Repeat the conversation to the daughter and just hope
   for the best.

3. You are making a sales presentation to a group of corporate
   executives in the plushest office you've ever seen. The hot
   enchillada casserole and egg salad sandwich you had for lunch
   react, creating a severe pressure. Your sphincter loses its control and you break wind in a most convincing manner causing
   3 water tumblers to shatter and a secretary to pass out. What
   you should do next is:

   _ a. Offer to come back next week when the smell has gone
   away.

   _ b. Point out their chief executive and accuse him of the
   act.

   _ c. Challenge anyone in the room to do better.

4. You are at a business lunch when you are suddenly overcome
   with an uncontrollable desire to pick your nose. Remembering
   this is definitely a "no-no," you:

   _ a. Pretend to wave to someone across the room and with
   one fluid motion, bury your forefinger in your nostril
   right up to the 4th joint.

___ b. Get everyone drunk and organize a nose-picking contest with a prize to the one who makes his nose bleed first.

___ c. Drop your napkin on the floor and when you bend over to pick it up, blow your nose on your sock.

5. After winning first prize for the most consumption at an all-night drinking party, you get home just in time to go to work. After arriving, you stagger to the men's room and spend the next half hour vomiting. As you're washing up at the sink, the sales training director walks up, blows his cigar in your face, and asks you to join him for drinks after work. You:

___ a. Look him straight in the eye and launch one last convulsion at the front of his Hart Schaffner & Marx suit.

___ b. Nail him right in the crotch, banking on the fact he'll never recognize your green face.

___ c. Grasp his hand and pump it until he pees in his pants.

6. You are at dinner with a customer and his wife (who looks like the regional runner-up of the Queen Kong look-alike contest). Halfway through dinner you feel a hand on your lap. Being resourceful, you:

___ a. Accidentally spill hot coffee in your lap.

___ b. Slip a note to the waiter to have your customer paged and see if the hand goes away when he does.

___ c. Excuse yourself and go to the men's room. If he follows, don't come out until your shorts rot.

7. You're on your way in to see your best account when your zipper breaks and you discover that you forgot to put your underpants on that morning. You decide to:

___ a. Call on the customer's secretary instead.

___ b. Explain you were just trolling for queers.

___ c. Buy a baggy raincoat and head for the nearest playground.

8. You've just returned from a trip to Green Bay, Wisconsin, in January and tell your boss that nobody but whores and football players live there. He then mentions that his wife is from Green Bay. You:

___ a. Ask what position she played.
___ b. Ask if she's still working the streets.
___ c. Pretend you're suffering from amnesia and don't remember your name.

87. Examination for Applicants as Reporters

Not all the tests transmitted by means of the office copier require the same degree of reader effort. The following test for prospective newspaper reporters provides the answers to the questions asked. By so doing, the test parody calls attention to the journalistic propensity to dwell upon such human tragedies as death, illness, and violent crime, and to describe such events in trite, tabloid terms. This text was collected in Berkeley in 1976.

Examination for Applicants as Reporters—
San Francisco Examiner
(Do not look at answers until you have finished writing.)

1. You are sent to a college commencement exercise to interview a representative graduate. You choose:

2. A sophomore girl at a local high school is found bludgeoned to death in a vacant lot. Knowing only this, you understand that your story will describe her as:

3. A police officer with a known record of brutality shotguns a 5-year-old black child for fleeing from the scene of a broken gumball machine. In your story, you will emphasize:

4. A charter airplane carrying 486 foster children to Disneyland crashes, killing them all. In your lead, you inform the readers that:

5. You have attended a press conference at which the mayor appears in a velvet tee shirt, blue golf slacks, and color-coordinated socks and tennis shoes. He tells a few ethnic jokes and announces that he will leave his wife to have two sex change operations and marry a hermaphrodite. You run to the hall and:

6. You interview a blind, paralyzed 105-year-old woman whose only sound is the gurgle of her saliva tube. You describe her as:

7. After months in a coma, a 14-year-old choir boy stricken on Easter Sunday undergoes experimental brain surgery and revives. Your story observes that this:

8. A highly regarded French intellectual, known for his perceptive though intricate analyses of international monetary problems, will hold a press conference in two days. With this much warning, you know:

9. Circumstances give you the ideal front-page story for Mother's Day:

10. On Sunday's front page column, "Pop" refers to:

–0–

1. The one with leukemia.
2. The most popular and pretty girl in her class.
3. The child's Communist associations.
4. This is tragic.
5. Agree with the Chronicle reporter to kill the story.
6. Alert.
7. Answers the prayers of millions.
8. That you don't have to prepare. You will be assigned instead to write a feature about a Mill Valley youth who raised a legless pelican from infancy.
9. A quiet, mild-mannered gardener who has lived with his strong-principled mother all his life hacks her to death and feeds her to the poodles.
10. God.

88. Physics Examination Problem

The validity of tests is an important issue. The plight of a creative student is the subject of the following account of one particular problem on a physics examination. This item, which is also found in oral tradition, was reported in R. L. Loeffelbein, "How Many Right Answers Are There?" in *California Teacher* for January 1977. (For another version entitled "The Barometer," see YD, 38.)

A physics teacher at Washington University in St. Louis was about to give a student a zero for the student's answer to an examination problem. The student claimed he should receive a perfect score, if the system were not so set up against the student. Instructor and student agreed to submit to an impartial arbiter, Dr. Alexander Calandra, who tells the story.

The examination problem was: "Show how it is possible to determine the height of a tall building with the aid of a barometer."

The student's answer was, "Take the barometer to the top of the building, attach a long rope to it, and lower the barometer to the ground. Then, bring it back up, measuring the length of the rope and barometer. The lengths of the two together is the height of the building."

I, as arbiter, pointed out that the student really had a strong case for full credit since he had answered the problem completely and correctly. On the other hand, of course, full credit would contribute to a high grade for the student in his physics course, and a high grade is supposed to certify that the student knows some physics, a fact that his answer had not confirmed. So it was suggested the student have another try at answering the problem.

He was given six minutes to answer it, with the warning this time that the answer should indicate some knowledge of physics. At the end of five minutes, he had not written anything. Asked if he wished to give up, he said no, that he had several answers and he was just trying to think which would be the best. In the next minute he dashed off this answer. "Take the barometer to the top of the building. Lean over the edge of the roof, drop the barometer, timing its fall with a stopwatch. Then, using the formula $S = \frac{1}{2} at^2$, calculate the height of the building."

When You're up to Your Ass in Alligators . . .

At this point, I asked my colleague if he gave up and he conceded. The student got nearly full credit.

Recalling the student had said he had other answers, I asked him what they were.

"Well," he said, "you could take the barometer out on a sunny day and measure the height of the barometer, the length of its shadow, and length of the building's shadow, then use simple proportion to determine the height of the building. And there is a very basic measurement method you might like. You take the barometer and begin to walk up the stairs. As you climb, you mark off lengths of the barometer along the wall. You then count the number of marks to get the height of the building in barometer units.

"Of course, if you want a more sophisticated method, you can tie the barometer to the end of a string, swing it as a pendulum and determine the value of 'g.' The height of the building can, in principle, be calculated from this.

"And," he concluded, "If you don't limit me to physics solutions, you can take the barometer to the basement and knock on the superintendent's door. When he answers, you say, 'Mr. Superintendent, I have here a fine barometer. If you will tell me the height of this building, I will give you this barometer.'"

Finally, he admitted that he even knew the correct textbook answer—measuring the air pressure at the bottom and top of the building and applying the formula illustrating that pressure reduces as height increases ($p = p_0 e^y$)—but that he was so fed up with college instructors trying to teach how to think, instead of showing him the structure of the subject matter, that he had decided to rebel.

For my part, I seriously considered changing my grade to unequivocal full credit.

89. Final Exam

The experience of taking a comprehensive final examination is one shared by students everywhere. The following parody of essay-type final examination questions has been collected in North Carolina, Indiana, Texas, Oregon, and California. It undoubtedly also circulates in the other states. It has also appeared in newsletters for educators and other professional groups. The following version was collected in California in 1975. (For nearly identical versions from England, see YWIW, [86], and TCB, 84–85.)

INSTRUCTIONS: Read each question carefully. Answer all questions. Time limit 4 hours. Begin immediately.

HISTORY: Describe the history of the papacy from its origins to the present day, concentrating especially, but not exclusively, on its social, political, economic, religious, and philosophical impact on Europe, Asia, America, and Africa. Be brief, concise, and specific.

MEDICINE: You have been provided with a razor blade, a piece of gauze, and a bottle of alcohol. Remove your appendix. Do not suture until your work has been inspected. You have fifteen minutes.

PUBLIC SPEAKING: 2500 riot-crazed students are storming the classrooms. Calm them. You may use any ancient language except Latin or Greek.

BIOLOGY: Create life. Estimate the differences in subsequent human culture if this form of life had developed 500 million years earlier, with special attention to its probable effect on the English parliamentary system. Prove your thesis.

MUSIC: Write a piano concerto. Orchestrate and perform it with flute and drum. You will find a piano under your seat.

PSYCHOLOGY: Based on your knowledge of their works, evaluate the emotional stability, degree of adjustment, and repressed frustrations of each of the following: Alexander of Aphrodisias,

Rameses II, Gregory of Nyssa, Hammurabi. Support your evaluation with quotations from each man's work, making appropriate references. It is not necessary to translate.

ASTRONOMY: Describe the universe and give 2 examples.

SOCIOLOGY: Estimate the sociological problems which might accompany the end of the world. Construct an experiment to test your theory.

ENGINEERING: The disassembled parts of a high powered rifle have been placed on your desk. You will also find an instruction manual, printed in Swahili. In 10 minutes a hungry Bengal tiger will be admitted to the room. Take whatever action you feel appropriate. Be prepared to justify your decision.

ECONOMICS: Develop a realistic plan for refinancing the national debt. Trace the possible effects of your plan in the following areas: Cubism, the Donatist controversy, the wave theory of light. Outline a method for preventing those effects. Criticize this method from all possible points of view. Point out the deficiencies in your point of view, as demonstrated in your answer to your last question.

POLITICAL SCIENCE: There is a red telephone on the desk beside you. Start World War III. Report at length on its socio-political effects, if any.

EPISTEMOLOGY: Take a position for or against truth. Prove the validity of your stand.

PHYSICS: Explain the nature of matter. Include in your answer an evaluation of the impact of the development of mathematics on science.

PHILOSOPHY: Sketch the development of human thought; estimate its significance. Compare with the development of any other kind of thought.

GENERAL KNOWLEDGE: Describe in detail. Be objective and specific.

Top Drawer Lore: Cartoons

No area of office copier folklore is richer than folk cartoons. Many are classics antedating the advent of modern means of rapid production, which have greatly facilitated the diffusion of these cartoons. It would be easy to devote an entire book to this important folklore form. Some of the cartoons frankly verge on the pornographic. A few readers may blanch at some of the examples we have included, but we have reluctantly excluded a number of items, for example, several showing explicit acts of cunnilingus, fellatio, and bestiality, which would almost certainly offend most readers.

In most cases, we present a single typical example. However, on occasion we demonstrate the traditionality or the range of variation of a particular folk cartoon by including more than one illustration. We wish to stress that whatever the origin of a particular cartoon may be, these cartoons are drawn and redrawn again and again. They are not the work of professional cartoonists. They bear no author's signature and they display multiple existence and variation, the hallmarks of folklore.

The content of folk cartoons parallels the themes found in the other genres of office copier folklore. The effect of the cartoons, however, is sometimes more striking because of the use of images. "A picture is worth a thousand words." The American version of an ancient Chinese proverb attests to the potency of pictures. It seems strange that this important form of folk art has not received critical attention from professional students of folklore. The dozen or so examples in UF barely scratched the surface of the many folk cartoons in circulation (see UFFC-PC). The sampling of folk cartoons presented here gives a reasonable indication of the remarkable richness of the tradition.

90. I Hate Poorly Organized Stampedes

For all the criticisms of the excesses of bureaucratic structures, Americans rely on a host of institutions to provide order. Rugged individualism may be admired as an ideal in the abstract, but it may be counterproductive in the context of a team effort. Even some outlaw or criminal behavior requires planning and careful organization to ensure a successful operation. A strike or a stampede cannot succeed unless the participants are moving in the same direction. The following drawing was collected in the office of the Anthropology Department of the University of California, Berkeley, in 1975.

91. God Bless Our Organization

The importance of organization to business efficiency is signaled by formal organization charts that show the hierarchical chain of command and the positions and responsibilities of key personnel. The disparity between ideal and real, theoretical and practical, often results in a different work pattern from that indicated by the organization chart. This is the subject of the following cartoon collected in Berkeley in 1977.

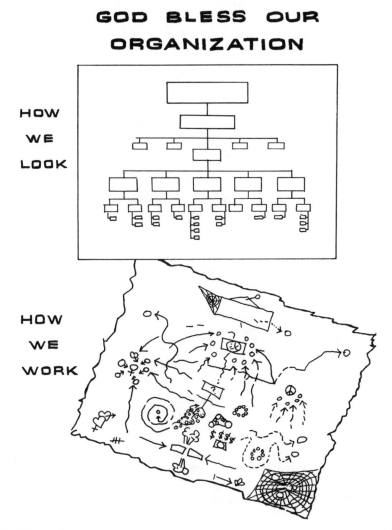

92. Organization Charts

Each institution may have its own special organizational idiosyncracies, which would presumably be reflected in that institution's formal organizational chart. The following folk cartoon, collected at the Research and Evaluation Department of the Oakland Public Schools in 1980, uses organizational charts as a means of articulating stereotypes ranging from national and ethnic slurs to parodies of such institutions as the Vatican, the Pentagon, and Women's Lib. (For another version, see YD, 6.)

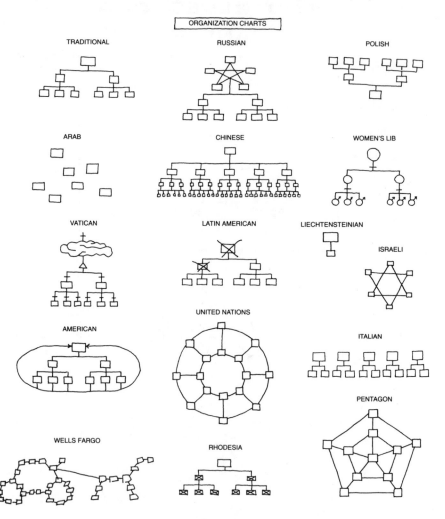

When You're up to Your Ass in Alligators . . .

93. You Want It *When?*

Part of the strain of office work is caused by the constant pressure to meet deadlines or to service individuals with competing demands. Bosses may ask for immediate action, but it is impossible for every request to be given first priority. An underling might like to protest unreasonable requests, but he may be fearful of doing so. By posting the following folk cartoon, he can make his point without having to address himself to individual work orders. The following version was collected in 1976 from an office at the University of San Francisco. (For two additional versions, see UFFC-PC, 102–3. For another, see YD, 4. For a German version, see IK, 78. The caption in the Anglo-American versions was used as the title for the English collection YWIW. For an English version, see OG2, 51.)

YOU WANT IT WHEN?

94. I Quit!!

One way of expressing dissatisfaction or protesting working conditions is to resign. Few are willing to take this ultimate and economically perilous step. Yet many employees surely have the urge to throw caution to the winds and to say just once "to hell with it!" or, equally common, "piss on it!" The following folk cartoon is extremely popular and has been collected coast to coast. The version presented here is from Oakland in 1974. Legman (NLM, 745) alludes to a 1965 version. The German version inspired an article and a book by folklorist Uli Kutter. See "'Ich Kündige': Zu einer Folklore der Imponderabilien," *Zeitschrift für Volkskunde* 77 (1981): 243–61, and IK, 8.

95. I'm So Happy Here

Some employees lack the nerve to complain and they prefer to suffer in silence. The frog in the following popular cartoon declares happiness, but his facial expression, his slumping posture, and his empty desk connote weariness, boredom, and general apathy. The frog's having his own desk and an executive swivel chair suggests he holds a managerial white-collar position. Even if there is no challenging work, he is obliged to man his post. One of the hardest things to do in any office is to look busy in the absence of any assigned duties. The following version of the frog cartoon was collected in Oakland in 1974. (For five additional versions, see UFFC-PC, 125–29.)

When You're up to Your Ass in Alligators . . .

96. The Mushroom

The plight of the office worker who feels uninformed and victimized is likened to a mushroom in a popular cartoon. Each of the three following versions collected in California in 1975–76 shows variation in both the drawing and the text. That such a simple drawing and caption can manifest differences in detail—it is rare to find two identical versions—is one of the most fascinating aspects of office copier folklore. (For five additional versions all of whose texts begin with "I must be a mushroom," see UFFC-PC, 107–11. For an English version, see OG2, 5).

I THINK I must be a mushroom. Everybody keeps me in the dark and feeds me bullshit.

I am a mushroom
I must be a mushroom
They always keep me
in the dark and
feed me bullshit

When You're up to Your Ass in Alligators . . .

I THINK I AM A MUSHROOM,

BECAUSE THEY KEEP ME IN THE DARK AND FEED ME BULLSHIT!

97. Recycling Has Gone Too Far

As awareness of the limitedness of resources has increased, Americans have come to realize how wasteful they are. Centers for the collection of newspapers, glass containers, aluminum cans, and other materials that can be processed for re-use have sprung up. The following folk cartoon presents the subject of waste products in general by depicting a scene concerned with body wastes. However, in the cartoon it is the paper rather than the feces that is presumably to be re-used. The pun on *cycle* is clear from the use of bicycle pedals. Some versions of this cartoon have an ethnic slur added by labeling the invention a Polish (or Italian) paper recycler. This version was collected in Oakland in 1974. (For three additional versions, see UFFC-PC, 14–16.)

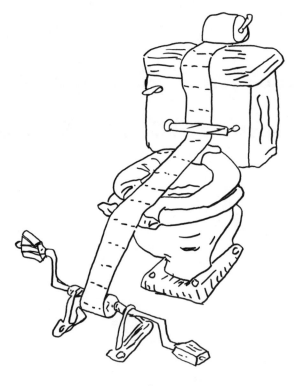

RECYCLING HAS GONE TOO FAR

When You're up to Your Ass in Alligators . . .

98. The Work Week

One of the most popular dog characters is Snoopy of Charles Schulz's *Peanuts* comic strip. In one of the few nonobscene folk cartoons derived from *Peanuts* characters, the daily morale and energy level of the office worker are depicted. In the first version, collected in Los Angeles in 1976, Snoopy starts work on Monday full of vim and vigor. However, he is played out by Tuesday and is still so exhausted by Wednesday as to remain unmoved in the face of a thunderstorm. By Thursday the thought of the coming weekend has revived him and by Friday he is smiling at the prospect of "kicking up his heels" (cf. the folk acronym TGIF: Thank God, It's Friday). The second version collected at the Lowie Museum of Anthropology at the University of California, Berkeley, in 1974, shows a different sequence inasmuch as there is a gradual decline in energy from Monday to Friday. The contrast between the work week and the weekend is the difference between work and play. (For a version like our second one, see UFFC-PC, 33.)

99. Fly United

Advertising slogans offer a fertile field for folk improvisation. The slogan "Fly United" associated with a major airline provides the impetus for the following folk cartoon. Appearing in wallet card, notepad, and full-page cartoon forms, the pair of flying creatures, usually ducks, show variation in detail and expression. In one variant, the participants are bees. Because the most common colloquial euphemism for the basic data about sex and reproduction refers to "the birds and the bees," the choice of flying creatures is not surprising. The reason for ducks, as opposed to other kinds of birds, might have to do with rhyme. "Fuck a duck" is a traditional exclamation and in rhyming slang, "lame duck" and "goose and duck" have been reported as substitute phrases for *fuck*. See Julian Franklyn, *A Dictionary of Rhyming Slang*, 2d ed. (London: Routledge and Kegan Paul, 1961), pp. 71, 90. The first version is from ISR and is dated 1971; the second is from Kokomo, 1976; the third was collected at Hughes Aircraft Company in El Segundo, California, in 1968; and the fourth was collected in Indianapolis in 1976.

When You're up to Your Ass in Alligators . . .

FLY   UNITED

FLY UNITED

When You're up to Your Ass in Alligators . . .

100. The Story of Twenty Toes Told in Twenty Minutes

The influence of comic strips is evident in a classic series of drawings showing the positions of a couple's feet in bed. The series may consist of as few as four or as many as eight panels. Titles of versions not shown here include: "The 'Tail' of Twenty Toes Told in Twenty Minutes" (which has as a closing caption "The End of the Tail") and "A Story without Words." We have presented six versions to show variations. The first version was collected in San Francisco in 1944. The other versions are from ISR. The second, in silhouette style, is from New York City, 1962. The third and fourth versions are from Chicago, collected in 1946. The fifth version is interesting not only for its length but for its title, its pagination (indicating it may have circulated in booklet form), and the use of clock faces. Finally, an ISR (1947) cartoon version of a common comic toast is presented inasmuch as it reflects a similar theme. For a brief discussion of the metonymic use of feet to represent coitus, see Legman, RDJ, 494. For German examples of this item, see IK, 95.

RADIO NEWS

STATION "JAZZ" ON THE AIR

ONE TUBE OSCILLATING

ERECTING AERIAL   TUNING IN   RECEIVING   SIGNING OFF

        When You're up to Your Ass in Alligators . . .

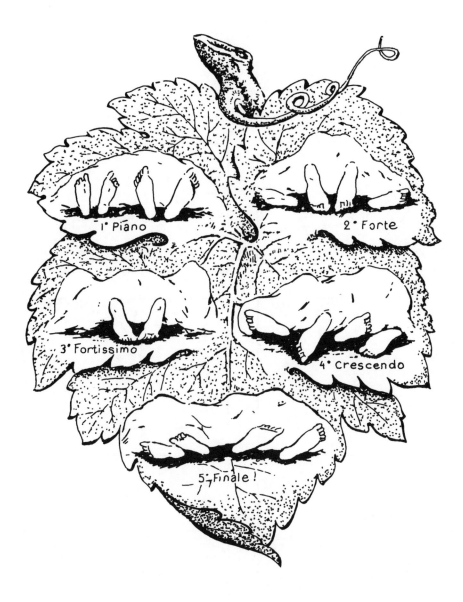

When You're up to Your Ass in Alligators . . .

Here's to moments of sweet repose,
   It's tummy to tummy and toes to toes
But after that moment of sweet delight
   It's fanny to fanny the rest of the night.

101. Old Lady Hitchhiker

The digitus impudicus is one of the most common folk ges-
tures in the United States, but until fairly recently it was used
primarily by males to other males. In 1976 Vice President Rockefeller surprised the media by responding to a group of hecklers
with this well-known gesture. A picture of the vice president
making the gesture was on the front page of almost every major
newspaper in America.

In hitchhiking custom, the finger used to indicate a ride is
desired is the thumb. There is even an expression "to thumb a
ride" referring to hitchhiking. In the following folk cartoon, an
elderly grandmotherly type is shown venting her anger at a motorist who has passed her by. She is presumably on her way back
to her car with a full can of gas. The cartoon may also be expressing the folk's response to the energy crisis (or to the temporary
Arab embargo on shipments of oil to the United States in 1973).
The cartoon, which circulated in an office at San Francisco International Airport, was collected in Menlo Park, California, in
1974. For another cartoon based on the same gesture, see "The
Finger," UF, 154–56 and UFFC-PC, 90.

102. The Last Great Act of Defiance

How one meets death is part of the image of the hero in American culture. One should not succumb without a struggle, but ideally one should be brave and courageous right up to the end, no matter how ferocious or dangerous an adversary may appear. This desideratum is depicted in the following folk cartoon. The first version was collected in California in 1976, the second in Kokomo in 1976, and the third in Berkeley in 1977. (For an additional version, see UFFC-PC, 89. For a version from England, see TCB, 2.)

When You're up to Your Ass in Alligators . . .

DEFIANCE!

103. Italian (Polish) Calculator

The phenomenal growth of the digital calculator industry has offered an inexpensive and easy-to-operate mechanical aid for computation. A common ethnic slur, which has been collected coast to coast, suggests that Italians (or Poles) have devised their own variety of this sophisticated device. The first version was collected in Fremont, California, in 1976; the second, with its addition of the razor blade to clear or erase, was collected the same year in South Windsor, Connecticut. (For two additional versions, see UFFC-PC, 4–5. For other versions of Italian and Polish cartoon ethnic slurs, see UF, 174–79; UFFC-PC, 2–30. In England, the calculator is Irish. For "the Shamrock pocket calculator," see OG2, p. 70.)

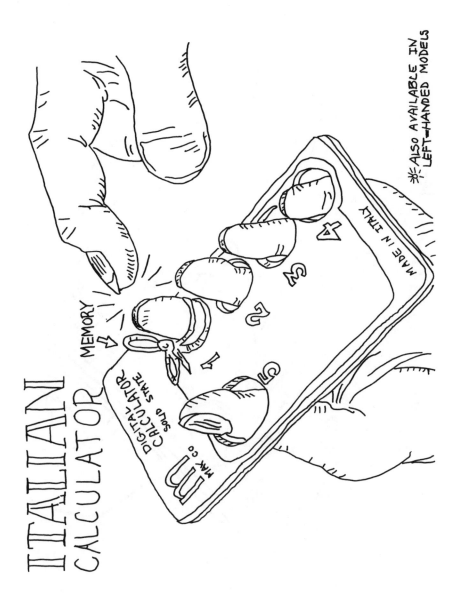

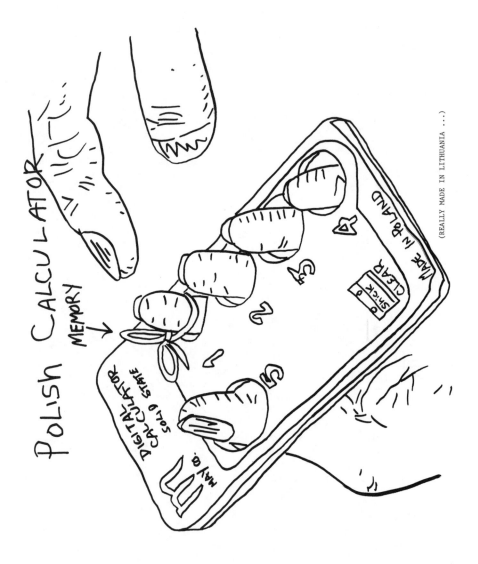

POLISH CALCULATOR

MEMORY

DIGITAL CALCULATOR SOLID STATE

CLEAR

MADE IN POLAND

(REALLY MADE IN LITHUANIA ...)

104. Travel Poland by Rail

More common than calculations in Polish and Italian jokes are miscalculations of considerable variety. Each of the three following folk cartoons mocks the alleged ineptitude of Poles and Italians. The lack of an ethnic group label in the second cartoon suggests that it is human fallibility in general that is the real subject of this type of joke. Despite the undeniable advances in modern technology, dams do break, bridges do fall, and unsinkable ships do sink. The cartoons simply give a concrete form to the worst imaginable engineering nightmares. The first example was collected from a bulletin board at the Naval Air Station in Alameda, California, in 1973. The second was collected in Oakland in 1974 and the third in Berkeley in 1976.

When You're up to Your Ass in Alligators . . .

Get it right the first time!

105. Polish Maternity Ward

The Polish stereotype applies to women as well as men. In the following cartoon, the prospective mother treats parturition as a child treats a loose tooth. Supposedly, a child with a loose tooth would attach a piece of string to the tooth and to a doorknob. The opening of the door was expected to extract the tooth. The lack of proper medical care during childbirth is of course no joke. But one wonders why in this Polish joke the folk did not put "push" rather than "pull" on the outside of the door. As in many of these ethnic slurs, the Italian appears almost as often as the Pole. The third example shows a more brutal technique, perhaps reflecting that it is typically a male obstetrician who has the female assume a position comfortable for him rather than for her. The first version is from the Indiana University Folklore Archives; the second was collected in Clairton, Pennsylvania, in 1976; the third was collected in Kokomo in 1976. (For three additional examples of our first version, see UFFC-PC, 19–21; see also Michael J. Preston, "Xerox-Lore," *Keystone Folklore* 19 [1974]:14.)

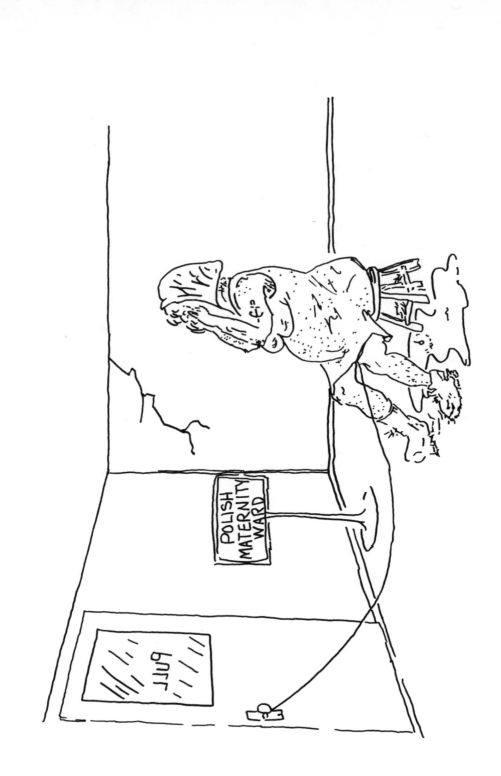

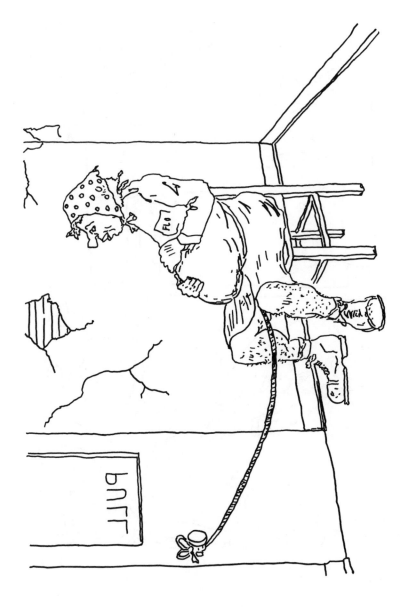

DAGO DELIVERY ROOM

Polish Delivery Room!

Dr. JANIAK

106. System Been Down Long?

Death as well as birth is depicted in folk cartoons. In this example, collected in 1982 from a buyer of young boys' clothes for a major department store chain in San Jose, California, it is the modern computer and its occasional baleful influence that is at issue. Computer technology has truly revolutionized the business world, and it is difficult to conceive of large corporations without bigger and better computers in their offices. The manufacture of relatively inexpensive models suitable for home use has made it possible for individuals as well as small companies to take advantage of the rapid handling of data storage and retrieval facilitated by computers. At the same time, man's increased dependence upon such technology has seemingly made him a veritable prisoner of the technology. One has only to visit a bank or a travel agency at a time when "the computers are down" to appreciate the frustration of both workers and clients under such circumstances. The computers may be out of commission for minutes, hours, or days. It is this unhappy situation which has inspired the following cartoon.

When You're up to Your Ass in Alligators . . .

107. A Round Tuit

Sometimes delay is unavoidable; sometimes it is not. Many reasons are given for delay, reasons such as overwork, low priority, and insufficient time. Typically, a promise may be given to complete the work at some future though rarely designated date. As protest against one of the most common delaying idioms, the following ingenious folk device has been invented. It appears to have swept the country during the late 1970s.

Our earliest version is dated 1975. The first version below was collected in Berkeley in 1976; the second was collected at Kaiser Center in Oakland the same year. (For another version, see UFFC-TB, 38. For versions from England, see YWIW, [30]; and TCB, 74.)

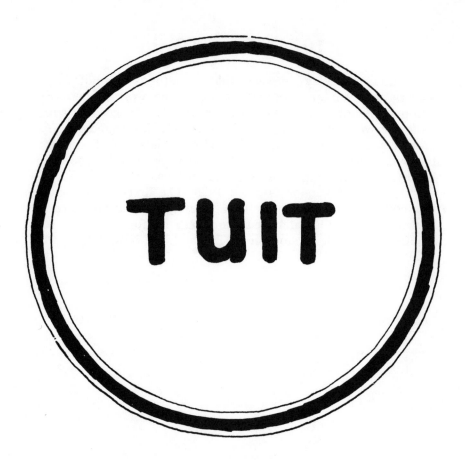

THIS IS AN INDISPENSABLE ITEM FOR EVERYBODY. FOR YEARS, PEOPLE HAVE BEEN SAYING, "I'LL DO IT AS SOON AS I GET A ROUND TUIT."

THE ABOVE IS A ROUND TUIT. CUT IT OUT, KEEP IT HANDY, AND YOU WILL HAVE NO MORE TROUBLE GETTING ALL THOSE EXTRAS DONE. YOU FINALLY GOT A ROUND TUIT!

When You're up to Your Ass in Alligators . . .

A ROUND TUIT

THIS IS A TUIT! GUARD IT WITH YOUR LIFE AS TUITS ARE HARD TO COME BY, ESPECIALLY THE ROUND ONES. THIS IS AN INDISPENSABLE ITEM. IT WILL HELP YOU BECOME A MUCH MORE EFFICIENT WORKER. FOR YEARS WE HAVE HEARD PEOPLE SAY, "I'LL DO THIS AS SOON AS I GET *A ROUND TUIT.*" NOW THAT YOU HAVE ONE, YOU CAN ACCOMPLISH ALL THOSE THINGS YOU PUT ASIDE UNTIL YOU GOT *A ROUND TUIT.*

108. Port-a-Dog

The unfettered imagination of the folk can be observed in the areas of design and mechanical invention. No part of the American scene is exempt from the creative attention of ingenious entrepreneurs. Pets, for example, have stimulated an extensive industry ranging from pet foods to pet cemeteries. One practical problem for the American who travels is what to do with his pet. He can either board him at a kennel or doggy motel, the comfort and cost of which can rival those of human accommodations, or he can take the pet with him. Special containers have been devised to transport a variety of animal life on airplanes. The following item collected in San Jose, California, in 1977, displays a simple device that serves not only to carry one's pet, but also to solve the problem resulting from a lack of rest room facilities for dogs on most airplanes. (For a German version, see IK, 82. For an English version referring to an Irish dog carrier, see TCB, 111–12.)

When You're up to Your Ass in Alligators . . .

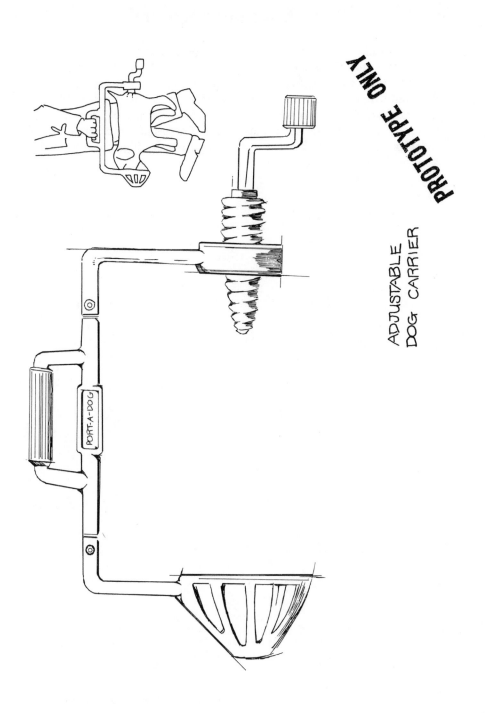

PROTOTYPE ONLY

ADJUSTABLE
DOG CARRIER

PORT-A-DOG

109. Frog Legs Special

Animals that are eaten are rarely pets. Even so, members of western industrial societies prefer not to think of the butchering of the meat they consume. The following cartoon collected in Oakland in 1981 depicts a confrontation between diners in a restaurant and their food source. Frog legs, a delicacy of French cuisine, is rarely on the American menu. The question does arise as to what happens to the rest of the frog once its legs are removed. (For an English version, see TCB, 114.)

When You're up to Your Ass in Alligators . . .

110. Now I Are One!

The increase of mass higher education has led some critics to complain about what they consider to be lower standards and cheap degrees. College graduates who are barely equipped with minimal skills have called into question the quality of the entire system of higher education. By the same token, the knowledge explosion has led to greater and greater specialization, particularly in scientific and technical fields. Part of the folk stereotype of the engineer, for example, is that he is scarcely literate. The first version was collected from Pacific Gas and Electric Company in San Francisco in 1976. The second was collected in Buffalo in 1977. (One informant reported seeing a version of this cartoon in Columbus, Ohio, in 1957.) For an English version, see YWIW, [47]; for a German version, see IK, 75.

SIX MUUCE UGO ICUTNT
EVN SPEL INJUNEER —
AN NOW I ARE ONE ●●●

When You're up to Your Ass in Alligators . . .

Twice Over Lightly:
The Double Entendre

Double entendres can be based on one-word puns but more often they consist of elaborate extended conceits. No fewer than sixteen examples of this popular form of copier folklore were reported in UF. The additional examples presented here show the rich variety of this genre. Most constitute thinly disguised descriptions of sexual activity. Freudians are commonly accused of interpreting nearly everything in sexual terms. These double entendres suggest that the folk themselves miss few opportunities to transform innocent activities into suggestive conduct. The repetitiveness of the sexual themes seems to demonstrate a narrowness of imaginative scope, but the repetition emphasizes the importance of sexuality in American culture. Specifically, for many decades Americans felt constrained to describe sexual behavior in euphemistic disguise; this attests to the repressive heritage from the Puritans to the Victorians.

Many of the items reported here appear to be at least thirty or more years old. It is doubtful that a society that permitted free discussion of sexuality would have produced so many examples of this genre of folklore. The amount of folklore clustering around a particular topic is surely related to the degree of anxiety felt by members of a society. The more the anxiety, the more the folklore. With more openness concerning sexuality, there is some question whether these materials will continue to appeal to the same degree as they evidently have to date. But not all Americans accept what they consider to be the lack of appropriate restraints on sexual behavior and expressive materials, such as films, popular literature, and art depicting such behavior. For sections of the populace who for one reason or another—religious convictions, strict parental regulation, and so forth—continue to regard sexuality as taboo or evil and sinful, the double entendre is likely in the future to provide a titillating and amusing outlet for dealing with sexual themes.

111. Have You Heard the One About . . . ?

The office copier facilitates the transmission of short jokes and the more elaborate long jokes. There are hundreds of these one-liners. Many of them depend on puns that produce short double entendres. Puns are definitely more effective in oral tradition than in written. The oral pun preserves the ambiguity. The written pun normally spells out—literally—one of the choices: "The two angels who got kicked out of heaven for trying to make a profit." On the other hand, the copying of lists of "punning rhetorical questions" results in the wholesale transmission of more examples than is common in the purely oral context. A raconteur might recite a half dozen or so texts but is unlikely to deliver three dozen or more in succession. The following compilation was collected in the Bay Area in 1976.

HAVE YOU HEARD THE ONE ABOUT

The two old maids that got on a drunk and nearly killed him?
The careless canary that did it for a lark?
The truck driver who broke his arm when he pulled out to avoid
    a child and fell off the divan?
The sleepy bride who couldn't stay awake for a second?
The All-American tom cat that made forty-seven yards in one
    night?
The traffic statistics which show that 90% of all people are
    caused by accidents?
The romantic mixed up stork that took a shine to a white girl?
The girl who wanted to be a bubble dancer, but her father said
    "No soap"?

The man that stole his neighbor's wife, piece by piece?

The foreign virgin that didn't come across?

The high-salaried movie producer that was always trying to make a little extra?

The girl who decided to get a mink fur the same way minks do?

The milkman who was late on the third floor because he got a little behind on the second?

The girl who went to her boy friend's apartment for a midnight snack, but all she got was a tid bit?

The man about town who rented an apartment just big enough to lay his head and a few intimate friends?

The man who wouldn't practice birth control, and now they call him "papa"?

The farmer that couldn't keep his hands off his wife so he fired them?

The modern Cinderella who turns into a motel every night?

The cow that got a divorce because she got a bum steer?

The peculiar contractor that had his house made upside down?

The absent minded nurse who made the patient without disturbing the bed?

The fellow who bought his girl a bicycle, and now she peddles it all over town?

The woman who lived in Florida all her life but never had a palm on her place?

The old maid that found a tramp under her bed, and her stomach was on the bum all the rest of the night?

The chickens that ate racing forms and now they're laying odds?

The fellow who lost his girl friend, he forgot where he laid her?

The girl who was a wall flower at the dance, but a dandelion in the grass?

The two angels that got kicked out of heaven for trying to make a profit?

The drive-in theater manager who decided if business got any better he would start showing movies?

The two peanuts that took a walk in the woods—one was assaulted?

The recent survey on cigarettes which found that 90% of the men that try Camels still prefer women?

The woman who was looking for a young man because she didn't like to feel old age creeping up on her?

The fellow who got up one morning and decided it looked so nice out he would leave it out?

The Sunday School teacher who chased her boy friend all over the church and finally caught him by the organ?

The fellow who descended from a long line his mother once heard?

The pregnant nurse whose theme was Witch Doctor?

The two queer judges that tried each other?

The shotgun marriage? It was a case of wife or death?

The butcher who got a little behind in his work? He backed into the meat slicer.

A bird in the hand is sure messy.

The farmer's daughter who was sent home from the fair—she couldn't keep her calves together?

The madam that changed place with one of the girls because she was bored with administration?

The executive who was so old that when he chased his secretary around the desk, he couldn't remember why?

The newlyweds who sneaked out of the wedding reception early to go up and get their things together?

The guy that fell into the cesspool—he couldn't swim but he went through all the movements?

The girl that wanted to make an impression on her new boy friend, so she put on her low cut dress to show him a thing or two?

The expert who could tell a girl sardine from a boy sardine by watching to see what can they came out of?

The bee that broke his leg—he fell off his honey?

The eager bride to be that came walking down the aisle?

The little boy who wanted a watch for Christmas—so they let him?

The new girl at the airplane factory who thought a tail assembly was a company picnic?

The colored man who saw his girl friend in a sack dress and said, "Honey, is you in fashion or is we in trouble?"

The above text is representative. Another version collected at Pacific Gas and Electric in San Francisco in 1976 has many of the same items with the following additions:

Have you heard the One About—

The pregnant skeleton—she didn't have the guts to say no?
The queer termite who ate his shack up?

When You're up to Your Ass in Alligators . . .

The Indian who didn't know heads from tails—you should see his scalp collection?

The State of Confusion—a bunch of queers at a wiener roast?

The plastic surgeon who hung himself?

For more examples in print, see Alan Dundes and Robert A. Georges, "Some Minor Genres of Obscene Folklore," *Journal of American Folklore* 75 (1962): 221–26; and Leopold Fectner, *American Wit and Gags* (New York: Vantage Press, 1969), pp. 114–18.

112. Potpourri

Other lists of short jokes make use of different genres, such as definitions. The following compilation collected in Clairton, Pennsylvania, in 1976, is typical. It contains many double entendres.

1. If you don't know the difference between a woman and a submarine, you've never been in a submarine.
2. If the girl next door forgets to pull down her shade, pull yours.
3. Said the two old maids to the magician, "Cut out the hokus and pokus."
4. The latest love ballad: "I used to kiss her on the lips, but it's all over now."
5. A gold digger is a girl who hates poverty worse than sin.
6. Know what they call a woman who doesn't practice birth control? A Mother!
7. A man who makes love in the morning is an idiot. After all, you never know what may turn up later in the day.
8. His secretary used to watch the clock—Now he's got her watching the calendar.
9. The meanest man in the world is the one who didn't tell his wife he was sterile until after she got pregnant.
10. After a wedding of mutual friends, the best man went out with the maid of honor, and boy did he get honor!
11. She used peroxide in her

bath water because she knew that on the whole gentlemen prefer blondes.

12. The difference between dark and hard is that it gets dark every night.

13. All this talk of a cold war we'd gladly trade for a hot peace.

14. It's a queer termite that goes for a woodpecker.

15. The man stopped his car and said to the girl hitch-hiker, "If I give you a ride what's in it for me?" And she said, "Dust, I've been walking all day."

16. Sounds in the night: "Daddy, if you get me a drink of water, I'll shake the bed for Mama."

17. The job application form said "SEX?" Sinful Sandra wrote, "Twice a week."

18. If a light sleeper sleeps lighter with the light on, does a hard sleeper sleep harder with a hard on?

19. Talk about a dumb blonde! She has to take off her sweater to count to two!

20. Witches don't have babies because their husbands have holloweenies.

21. Alimony—the screwing you get for the screwing you got.

22. Did you ever stop to think that if the Pilgrims had shot bob cats instead of turkeys for food, we'd be eating pussy for Thanks-giving?

23. She said she'd do anything for a mink coat, and now that she has it, she can't button it.

24. Girls, you'd better be using what Mother Nature gave you before Father Time takes it away!

25. They were married, and the first morning after he was awakened by her in-specting him and crying loudly. He asked her why she was crying and she sobbed, "Look, we almost used it all up the first night!"

26. Sex may be bad for one, but it's sure wonderful for two!

113. Biblical Facts

There is folklore in the Bible. It includes myths, folktales, legends, proverbs, and riddles. Sir James George Frazer's three-volume *Folklore in the Old Testament* is but one example of the scholarship. There is also folklore based on the Bible. For example, there are catechetical riddling questions that cannot be answered unless one possesses knowledge of biblical details. Who in the Bible speaks and yet goes to neither heaven nor hell?—Balaam's ass. Who was born once and died twice?—Lazarus. Part of the folklore based on the Bible is profane, to say the least. The following item from ISR uses biblical characters or events as a vehicle for double entendres.

Biblical Facts.

Who was the first Jockey? Adam. Why? Because he put Eve on the turf and entered her for the human race.

Who won the race? Eve, because she took the pole and kept it through the heat.

Who lost the race? Adam, because he broke and ran on the home stretch.

What three great men do we read of in the Bible who never sat on their shirt-tail?

Cain, because he was not Abel, and Balaam, because he had trouble with his ass, and Elijah was made ascend up.

Where do we first read of seduction in the Bible? It is where Abraham led Isaac to Mount Moriah, and took Aram in the bush.

What did Adam do when he discovered the difference between him and Eve? He split the difference, he raised Cain, and did it again when he got Abel.

114. Apartment for Rent

Sexual stereotypes include the female whose vagina is too large and the male whose organ is too small. See, for example, G. Legman's discussion of "The Overlarge Vagina" in NLM, 449–57. Legman astutely remarks that these two stereotypes are mutually reinforcing. A man rather than admitting his penis is inadequately sized says that the woman's vagina is too big. See RDJ,

377, 535. The following letter exchange collected from Concord, New Hampshire, in 1977, presents both stereotypes. (For another text involving a verbal duel between the sexes with the female triumphant, see UF, 207–9. For an English version, see TCB, 148.)

APARTMENT FOR RENT

A prosperous business man propositioned a beautiful chorus girl. She agreed to spend the night with him for $500.00. When he was ready to leave he told her that he didn't have the money with him, but he would have his secretary write a check for it and mail it to her, calling it "rent for apartment." On the way to the office he decided the whole thing wasn't worth the price he had agreed to pay, so he had his secretary send the following with a check for $250.00.

Dear Madam:
    Enclosed find check in the amount of $250.00 for rent on your apartment. I'm not sending the amount agreed, because when I rented the apartment, I was under the impression:
    1. It was never occupied.
    2. That there was plenty of heat.
    3. That it was small.
Last night I found it had been previously occupied, that there wasn't any heat, and that it was entirely too large.

Very Truly Yours,

Upon receipt of the note, the girl immediately returned the check for the $250.00 with the following:

Dear Sir:
    I cannot understand how you can expect a beautiful apartment to remain unoccupied. As for the heat, there is plenty of it if you know how to turn it on. As for the size—it is not my fault that you didn't have enough furniture to furnish it.

Very Truly Yours,

115. I've Been Married Nine Times

Occupations and their associated idioms provide the metaphorical ammunition for a litany of complaints about sexually inadequate males. Similar occupational double entendres found in card form have been presented earlier (see item 25). This version was collected in Oakland in 1974.

I've been married 9 times to 9 different men. Let me tell you what was wrong with each, except the last one.
1. My first husband was a musician—all he wanted to do was sing to it.
2. My second was a politician—all he did was make promises to it.
3. My third was a doctor—all he wanted to do was examine it.
4. My fourth was a psychiatrist—all he wanted to do was talk to it.
5. My fifth was a painter—all he wanted was to paint pictures of it.
6. My sixth was a policeman—all he wanted to do was keep it under lock & key.
7. My seventh was a cook—all he ever did was complain about how salty it was.
8. My eighth was a preacher—all he ever did was pray to it.
9. My ninth and last is the one I'm with now, and we get along fine. He's a mechanic. He tore it up the first night and has been working on it ever since.

116. Pipe Dream

Of all the double entendres that employ a catch device in which the item allegedly being described is finally revealed in the last line, the following is one of the oldest and most popular. One reason for its popularity may be that it is in rhyme. Titles of versions in ISR range from "The Tramp" to "Get It In!" and "A Difficult Task." The first version presented here dates from 1939 and was collected in San Francisco. The second version was collected from a woman in Washington, D.C., in 1976.

PIPE DREAM

A tramp once by a window passed
   And heard a maiden's voice
Speak to a man, and things she said
   To him seemed rather choice.

"Don't push so hard she said to him
   Don't jab around that way,
You'll get them right together, then
   Push easy when I say:

"There it is out again—it slips—
   They do not fit just right;
If the thing goes in straight you see
   'Twill fit quite snug and tight.

But the end seems a bit too big
   Perhaps the hole is too small
But if you twist and push that way
   It won't go in at all.

"Now let me fix it tight this time,
   When I say "now" you press,
There, easy "now!" or 'twill slip out
   And make an awful mess."

The tramp couldn't stand this longer
   So to peep in he strove,
And saw the maiden and the man
   Fitting pipe on the stove.

THE EAVESDROPPER

A tramp was leaning against the side
Close by the window frame,
Inside he heard some voices
And he heard a woman exclaim:

You can't do it that way
Don't you see that I can't wait?
You always let it wobble
Why don't you keep it straight?

If you do it this way
Then don't do it at all
I think yours is too big
If not, then mine's too small.

Let us try it this way once
But be careful of my dress
If you let it slip out
You'll make an awful mess

Just have a little patience
And you'll surely win,
See now you have it started
For Heaven's sake push it in.

The tramp got so excited
And for the window he dove
To see a man and woman
Fit a stove pipe to a stove.

117. Her First Experience

The following double entendre is also a catch playing on an innocent activity much like milking a cow or fitting a pipe to a stove. The first version, from ISR, was typewritten on a piece of paper bearing the letterhead "SOUTH PACIFIC FORCE of the United States Pacific Fleet, Headquarters of the Commander," which suggests that the item dates from World War II. The second and much shorter version was collected in 1970 in Logansport, Indiana. A third version is of special interest because it is in Spanish. Sent to us by folklorist Barbara Kirshenblatt-Gimblett, it was collected in Quito, Equador, in 1965. It attests to the international character and appeal of copier folklore. (For a German version, see IK, 96. For an English text of "milking a cow," see TCB, 168.)

"HER FIRST EXPERIENCE"

Slowly she leaned back and let her shapely legs relax, partly drawing up her dimpled knees.

She had put him off many times before—first one time and then another—always with constant fear in her heart. Someday she knew that she would give in to him—that someday he would get what he wanted out of her.

Yet, she too wanted it—wanted him to do it to her—but the constant fear and dread of it always held her back. She knew all along what would happen and now—now that the time had come, she resignedly gave herself up to him. After all, she was only a normal woman—she couldn't keep it forever—few women do. . . .

He, of course, had had this same experience with many other women before and she well realized that he would think nothing of it—but to her—this was the FIRST time!

But then it would be better with a man of experience. And thank God he was being kind and patient about it—assuring her that it would not hurt her too much the first time and that the after-effects would be most pleasant. . . .

Lightly and tenderly his fingers moved to touch it but she pulled away from him. Eventually, after plea and persuasion, his patience and consideration was rewarded—her tension relaxed and she permitted him to gently touch the tender spot.

As time went by he gradually straightened up, gazing at it as he worked himself into position. Her fear reawakened as she stared in horror at what he had in his hand. But this fear left her as she gazed up into his eyes and as he looked down at her with admiration and understanding, she slowly nodded consent. . . .

He was as tender and careful as he had promised he would be and although she moaned softly, she relaxed completely at his command and opened wider to him, drawing her knees even higher and laid back further so that he could go in with greater ease!

Her body quivered and as great, warm tears streamed down her cheeks, she cried aloud, "Oh my God, take it out—oh please take it out—you're killing me!"

Knowing and understanding, he smiled down upon her— "Don't cry my dear," he said, "Let it come out slowly, then it won't hurt."

Slowly he withdrew. She relaxed once more. . . .

"There," he said, "This tooth will never bother you again!"

THE END.

She lay back with a long drawn sigh allowing the muscles of her shapely legs to relax. Partly drawing up her shapely knees. For a moment she put it off. First one excuse then another resisting desperately all the time, but hoping deeply within her that the time had come. She was afraid of course, she knew he was experienced, and he was assuring her over and over again he would be careful. His hands violently fluttered to the spot where she ached. She realized that she was fascinated by the thing that he held in his hand. Her knees were drawn tightly together with fear. He was light and his hand went slowly to the spot which made chills go up and down her back. "No, no, no, don't do it." She couldn't stand it. It seemed like it was taking a day, but he had started only a minute ago. She felt the thing was coming. Her body grew limp and with a source of joy she lay back quietly; it was over. . . .
. . . . the tooth was out!

LA EMOCION EMBARGADORA

Con un suspiro se recostó ella; y, los múculos de su bien formado cuerpo, se aflojaron. Por un instante, se resistió a él; pero, deseando de todo corazón que no hiciera caso de sus protestas . . . Eso que le había quitado el sueño tantas noches era lo que ella quería; pero, ahora había llegado el momento y tenía miedo. Cierto, que él era un hombre con muchas experiencia; mas, era la primera vez.

Solos en esa piecita, ella se sintió nerviosa; él le ofreció no lastimarla. Le puso la mano sobre aquel lugar que ella escondíam mientras trataba de convencerla. Le quitó la mano, pero, él se la volvió a poner; y, esta vez, apretando. Ella dirigió los ojos, desmesuradamente abiertos, hacia la cosa que él tenía en la otra mano; sus protestas, se acentuaron, más todavía cuando él estuvo cercam sintiendo su aliento ajunto a su boca . . . La colmó de palabras dulces al oíd Le dijo; "Que era muy práctico y que no tuviera miedo, que no le iba a doler nada . . ."

Convencida, dejó que él maniobrara, aflojó los músculos y abrió bien para dar cabida a Aquello . . .

Su cuerpecito frágil se estremecía; quería luchar, pero sus fuerzas la abandonaban . . . Sintió correr algo caliente . . . SANGRE . . . S A N G R E. Una emoción viva la envolvió, entonces, gritó: No por favor . . . Ahora no aguanto más . . . No aguanto más . . . Déjeme por favor . . . Basta . . . Ah . . . AY . . . AY . . . No, No aguanto más. AH, AY, N O   M E   L A   S A Q U E   SE LO RUEGO. . . .

Parecía noche sin fin y ta sólo habían transcurrido unos pocos minutos, ya iba a concluir. Ella sintio viva emoción; su cuerpecito se estremecía, todavía, en contínuas convulsiones, una y otra vez ... Estaba extenuada ... Al cabo de un momento le dijo: "Acabé ..."; y, ella quedó satisfecha con los músculos laxos.

P O R   F I N   <u>E L DENTISTA LE HABIA SACADO LA MUELA</u>

118. Believe It or Not

An unusual but extremely popular example of a double entendre is constructed by arranging a sequence of advertising slogans. It was in circulation in the 1970s having been collected coast to coast. Frequently untitled, it has appeared with such titles as "An Embarrassing Coincidence of 'Do Not Believe in Signs'" (San Francisco, 1944); "The Month's Best Story" (Washington, D.C., 1973); and "Does Advertising Pay?" (New York City, 1962). For an earlier version in print, see Alan Dundes, "Advertising and Folklore," *New York Folklore Quarterly* 19 (1963): 143–51. The slogans in that version are: "The Gold Dust Twins Are Coming," "Sloan's Liniment to Prevent Swelling," "Williams Shaving Stick Did the Trick," and "Goodrich Rubber Would Have Prevented This Accident." In a Colorado version (UFFC-TB, 141), the slogans are almost identical with those in the text presented below. In a version reported by Legman (RDJ, 234–35) from a printed novelty card, 1940, but thought to date from 1920, the lines are: "The Gold Dust Twins Are Coming," "Johnson's Shaving Stick Did This," and "Kelly's Rubbers Could Have Prevented It." The version presented here circulated in the late 1930s in Cedar Rapids, Iowa.

BELIEVE IT OR NOT

A lady, about seven months pregnant, got onto a streetcar and sat down. She noticed the man opposite her smiling, so feeling humiliated, she changed her seat.

This time his smile changed into a grin, so she changed her seat again. The man seemed more amused than ever, so again she moved and immediately the man burst into laughter.

When You're up to Your Ass in Alligators ...

Feeling highly insulted, the woman complained to the conductor who had the man arrested. The case came up in court and the judge asked the man if he had anything to say, whereupon the man replied:

"Well, your honor, it was this way. When the lady got on the car I could not help but notice her condition, which in itself did not amuse me a bit, but when she sat down under a sign which read, "THE GOLD DUST TWINS ARE COMING," I had to smile; then when she moved and sat down under another sign which read, "SLOANS LINIMENT WILL REDUCE THAT SWELLING," I was forced to grin; then when she got up and sat down next time under a sign which read "WILLIAMS STICK DID IT," I thought that that was about the limit, which made me laugh out loud; and then when she got up again and sat down under a sign which read, "GOODYEAR RUBBER WOULD HAVE PREVENTED THIS ACCIDENT," I just lost control of myself.

Judge: "Case dismissed."

119. Thar's Gold in Them Thar Hills

In this double entendre, the reader is let in on the secret at the outset. This is in contrast with the catch double entendres in which the secret is withheld until the end. The version presented here is from ISR and was collected in Chicago in 1959. An alternative title is "A Mining Report." A version like the one below was in circulation in Kokomo in 1976.

Thar's Gold in Them Thar Hills

In a certain mining camp, Mrs. Brown presented her husband with a twelve-pound baby girl. Mr. Brown was so delighted he went to the newspaper office and told them he had found a twelve-pound nugget of gold. Naturally, the newspaper sent a reporter to get the full particulars and the following interview took place.

"Does Mr. Brown live here?"
"Yes. Won't you come in?"

"Is Mr. Brown home? I understand he found a twelve-pound nug-
    get of gold."
Seeing the joke, Mrs. Brown answered, "Yes sir."
"Can you show me the exact spot where it was found?"
"No, I am afraid not. Mr. Brown would object to that."
"Is the hole very far from here?"
"No. It's quite handy."
"Had Mr. Brown been working the claim long?"
"Just about ten months."
"Was he the first to work it?"
"Well, he thought he was."
"Was the work very difficult?"
"At first it was, but it is much easier now."
"Is the flow very plentiful?"
"It is sufficient to carry on his work."
"Has Mr. Brown gotten to the bottom yet?"
"No, I don't think so."
"Do you think he will find any more large nuggets?"
"Yes, if the claim is worked properly."
"Has the claim been worked since the last nugget was found?"
"No, but I told Mr. Brown I thought it was time he started."
"Would you help him in his work?"
"I would do my very best."
"Do you think he would sell his claim?"
"No, he finds too much pleasure working it himself."
"Would you mind showing the nugget to me?"
"Certainly not. Come in the next room."

The reporter was taken home in an ambulance.

120. Church Bulletin Misprints

Many versions of the following item contain a statement,
which says that the item appeared in a small town newspaper or
a church newsletter. The following version, collected in Clairton,
Pennsylvania, in 1976, lacks this statement. Local news coverage
of routine church activities is parodied.

This afternoon there will be a meeting in the North and South ends of the church. The children will be baptized at both ends.

Tuesday at 7:00 p.m. there will be an ice cream social hour and all ladies giving milk will please come by early.

Wednesday: The Ladies' Literary Society will meet. Mrs. Johnston will sing "Put Me in My Little Bed" accompanied by the pastor.

Thursday at 7:00 p.m. there will be a meeting of the "Little Mother's Club"; all ladies wishing to become Little Mothers will please meet the minister in his study at 6:30 p.m.

This being Easter Sunday we will ask Mrs. Brown to come forward and lay an egg on the altar.

The service will close with "Little Drops of Water." If some lady will quietly start, the rest of the congregation will follow.

On Sunday, a special collection will be taken up to defray the expense of the new carpet. Will all wishing to do something on the carpet, please come up and get a piece of paper.

* * * * * *

121. Father Murphy's Ass

This extremely popular item is variously titled. Titles include: "Father Murphy," "The Fund-Raising Problems (Program) of Father Murphy," "The Power of the Press," "The Meaning of Words," "Father Cleary's Donkey at Races." Known from coast to coast, the plight of Father Murphy has been in continuous tradition from the early 1940s if not before. The Catholic element is shown in the choice of dramatis personae: priest, nun, archbishop. Part of the humor depends on the profanation of the sacred. The following version was collected in Lafayette, California, in 1975. (For a 1953 version from New York City, see Legman, NLM, 817. See also UFFC-TB, 145.)

Father Murphy was a priest in a very poor parish. He asked for suggestions as to how he could raise money for his church. He was told that race owners always had money, so he went to a horse auction, but he made a very bad buy. The horse turned out to be a donkey.

However, he thought he might as well enter the donkey in a race and the donkey came in third and the headlines read: FATHER MURPHY'S ASS SHOWS. The Archbishop saw the paper and was greatly displeased.

The next day the donkey came in first and the headlines read: FATHER MURPHY'S ASS OUT IN FRONT. The Archbishop was up in arms and figured something had to be done because Father Murphy insisted on entering the donkey again and he came in second. Next morning the headlines read: FATHER MURPHY'S ASS BACK IN PLACE.

In order to prevent further scandal the Archbishop forbid the priest to enter the donkey in any more races. The headlines read: ARCHBISHOP SCRATCHES FATHER MURPHY'S ASS.

Seeing no alternative the Archbishop ordered Father Murphy to get rid of the donkey. He was unable to sell it, so he gave it to Sister Agatha for a pet. The next morning's headlines read: SISTER AGATHA GETS FATHER MURPHY'S ASS. The archbishop immediately ordered the good Sister to dispose of the animal.

The next day Sister Agatha sold the donkey at an auction for the sum of $10.00. Subsequently, the headlines read: SISTER AGATHA PEDDLES HER ASS FOR TEN DOLLARS.

The Archbishop was buried in three days.

122. The Isle of Man

A final example of double entendre also plays on the word *ass*. Dating from the early 1940s—Legman (NLM, 817) suggests the 1930s—the item has such titles as "The Ass," "Do You Know Your Own Ass?" and "An Essay on Donkeys." The version presented here was collected in San Francisco. Five versions from all over the United States are on deposit in the ISR.

"The Isle of Man"

Over near England there is a little island called the "Isle of Man." A very peculiar thing about the people on this island is that they do not believe in riding automobiles, and so they all ride donkeys, or what are commonly called asses. Every one has an ass. Some have just ordinary asses. Asses you wouldn't look at twice, while others have very extraordinary asses. Some have black asses and some have white asses. The Mayor, for instance, has an ass no one would like to look at even once, but the Mayor's wife has a beautiful ass. People who really know asses say she has one of the biggest and finest asses they have ever seen. Men often stop her as she goes to market, just to pat her ass. On Sunday, they all go to church on their asses. Some of the boys ride the girls' asses and some of the girls ride the boys' asses. One Sunday the preacher had to leave early following the service, so he thought he had better have his ass handy, so he tied it just outside the window. During the service a fire broke out, and of course, every one ran out to save his ass. The preacher jumped out of the window expecting to land on his ass, but there was a big hole there and he fell into the hole instead.

This only goes to prove that even a preacher doesn't know his ass from a hole in the ground.

Parity for Parody

Parody in the sense of caricaturing or making fun of an item or text already known to the audience is a common technique in folklore. There are parodies of folk songs, nursery rhymes, and literary poems, to mention a few of the most popular subjects. These parodies are often traditional ones so that the parodies are as much an example of folklore as the folklore that provided the point of departure for the parodies. In this volume previous examples of parodies are those of business and personal letters, greeting cards, comic strips, and advertisements.

To call attention to parody as one of the richest veins in American folk humor, we conclude our compilation by presenting parodies of forms ranging from recipes to elaborate fairy tales. Despite the importance of parody in American folklore, we find no book-length treatment of the subject. One can find only occasional brief discussions of parody, or of individual items such as "Mary had a little lamb." Many collections of literary parodies exist, but folkloristic parodies are yet to be investigated. The present collection of office copier folkloristic parodies ought surely to be an integral part of a definitive study.

For samples of literary (as opposed to folk) parodies, see Robert P. Falk, ed., *The Antic Muse: American Writers in Parody* (New York: Grove Press, 1955) and Burling Lowrey, ed., *Twentieth Century Parody, American and British* (New York: Harcourt, Brace and Company, 1960). For brief discussions of folklore parodies, see C. Grant Loomis, "Mary Had a Parody: A Rhyme of Childhood in Folk Tradition," *Western Folklore* 17 (1958): 45–51; Ed Cray, *The Erotic Muse* (New York: Oak Publications, 1969), pp. 86–89, 199; and Iona and Peter Opie, *The Lore and Language of Schoolchildren* (Oxford: Oxford University Press, 1959), pp.

87–97. Perhaps one of the best discussions of parody by a folklorist is Lutz Röhrich, *Gebärde, Metapher, Parodie* (Düsseldorf: Pädagogischer Verlag Schwann, 1967), pp. 115–221, which also includes a bibliography, pp. 229–31.

123. Turkey Stuffing

The recipe genre lends itself to parody. This text, collected in Palo Alto, California, about 1970, is typical. An alternative title noted on other versions is "Turkey Dressing." Perhaps one reason for this parody is the custom of pushing stuffing into a turkey through its posterior, a technique that, with a bit of imagination, could be interpreted as an anal erotic act. The first stanza of a folk song parody sung to the tune of "Frère Jacques" confirms such an imagery pattern:

> Next Thanksgiving,
> Next Thanksgiving,
> Save your bread,
> Save your bread;
> Stuff it up a turkey,
> Stuff it up a turkey;
> Eat the bird,
> Eat the bird.

(For another text of this item, entitled "Dressing Recipe," see UFFC-TB, 168.)

Turkey Stuffing

1 cup bread crumbs
2 eggs
½ tsp. cinnamon, allspice and sage (each)
1 cup of corn for popping
½ cup of milk

Rub inside of turkey with garlic and end of cut lemon. Mix all of the ingredients above together until well mixed.

Stuff loosely into cavity.

Cover bird with aluminum foil and set on top shelf of oven. Set at 400°.

Lift foil frequently and baste, but keep out of the way of the turkey because as soon as that corn starts to pop, it will blow the turkey's ass halfway across the room.

124. Thirty-Day Diet

As Americans have become more and more weight conscious, they have increasingly turned to exotic diets of all varieties. The unique diet presented in this text collected in San Francisco in 1974 features a mixture of commonly available substances with Spanish Fly, or cantharides, a preparation made from the blister beetle, believed to have strong aphrodisiac properties. Cantharides is reportedly used as a diuretic and as a genitourinary stimulant. Adolescent folklore includes many jokes and legends about the alleged use of Spanish Fly as an aphrodisiac. (For another version of the diet, see NLM, 361.)

30-DAY DIET

Take each day—¼ oz. Metrecal
¼ oz. Castor Oil
1 oz. Spanish Fly
1 pint Bourbon

At the end of 30 days you will be the skinniest, shittiest, sexiest, alcoholic in town.

125. Simplified 1040

Governments are notorious for their infinite varieties of forms. No form is better known to American taxpayers than the standard 1040 federal income tax form. Along with the increasing complexity of tax regulations and the forms associated with the regulations has been an attempt to simplify the tax return forms for wage earners of modest income. Typically these simplified forms are a single page. The following folk variation collected in Los Angeles in 1983 represents the ultimate in simplicity. (For an English version, see OG2, 83.)

Simplified 1040

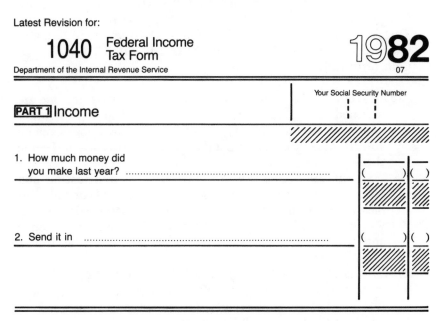

126. Horoscope

Another form that lends itself to parody is the horoscope in daily newspapers and other printed media. Despite the influence of science and technology, astrology and the occult continue to attract a considerable following. The idea is that individual human destiny is determined in large measure by one's birth date. Astrology is a fertile field for study by folklorists along with palmistry and fortune-telling. This parody of horoscopes was widely reported in 1975 and 1976. Titles include: "The Zodiac Never Lies!" and "Horror-Scope: What the Gypsy Was Afraid to Tell." The first version was collected in Des Moines, Iowa, in 1976. A second text, much less common, concerns a single astrological sign. It was collected in Alameda, California, in 1975. (For other versions of the first text, see UFFC-TB, 113, and YD, 16–17. For an English version, see TCB, 100–101. For further consideration of contemporary interest in the occult, see Marcello Truzzi, "The Occult Revival as Popular Culture: Some Random Observations on the Old and the Nouveau Witch," *Sociological Quarterly* 13 [1972]: 16–36.)

AQUARIUS (Jan. 20–Feb. 19) You have an inventive mind and are inclined to be progressive. You lie a great deal. On the other hand, you are inclined to be careless and impractical, causing you to make the same mistakes over and over again. People think you are stupid.

PISCES (Feb. 19–March 20) You have a vivid imagination and often think you are being followed by the CIA or FBI. You have a minor influence over your associates and people resent you for your flaunting of your power. You lack confidence and are generally a coward. Pisces people do terrible things to small animals.

ARIES (March 21–April 19) You are the pioneer type and hold most people in contempt. You are quick-tempered, impatient, and scornful of advice. You are not very nice.

TAURUS (April 20–May 20) You are practical and persistent. You have a dogged determination and work like hell. Most people think you are stubborn and bull-headed. Taurus people have B.O. and fart a lot.

GEMINI (May 21–June 20) You are a quick and intelligent thinker. People like you because you are bisexual. However, you are inclined to expect too much for too little. This means you are cheap. Geminis are known for commiting incest.

CANCER (June 21–July 22) You are sympathetic and understanding to other people's problems. They think you are a sucker.
You are always putting things off. That's why you'll never
make anything of yourself. Most welfare recipients are Cancer people.

LEO (July 23–Aug. 22) You consider yourself a born leader. Others
think you are pushy. Most Leo people are bullies. You are
vain and dislike honest criticism. Your arrogance is disgust-
ing. Leo people are thieves.

VIRGO (Aug. 23–Sept. 22) You are the logical type and hate disorder. This nit-picking is sickening to your friends. You are
cold and unemotional and sometimes fall asleep while making love. Virgos make good bus drivers.

LIBRA (Sept. 23–Oct. 22) You are the artistic type and have a
difficult time with reality. If you are a man, you are more
than likely queer. Chances for employment and monetary
gains are excellent. Most Libra women are good prostitutes.
All Librans have venereal disease.

SCORPIO (Oct. 23–Nov. 21) You are shrewd in business and cannot be trusted. You will achieve the pinnacle of success because of your total lack of ethics. Most Scorpios are mur-
dered.

SAGITTARIUS (Nov. 22–Dec. 21) You are optimistic and enthu-
siastic. You have a reckless tendency to rely on luck since
you lack talent. The majority of Sagittarians are drunks or
dope fiends. People laugh at you a great deal.

CAPRICORN (Dec. 22–Jan. 19) You are conservative and afraid of
taking risks. You don't do much of anything and are lazy.
There has never been a Capricorn of any importance. Capri-
corns should avoid standing still too long as a dog might
think you are a tree and piss on you.

People born under the sign of Sagittarius make excellent
cheapskates. If you were born on the 22nd you are one day older
than people born on the 23rd, but it doesn't matter—because you
are all cheapskates anyway. Your love life is governed by the distant planet Fringus, which is only three inches in diameter, and
you have a tendency to be shy when undressing out of doors. Your
lucky day is Dennis, your lucky color runs when laundered, and
your lucky number is MCVIII. You must fight your primary

weakness—delusions of adequacy. However, with concentration and dedication, you can become average. Financial matters for Sagittarians are always lousy, and you are unlucky at love and finding water. This birth sign is a veritable hex, historically filled with gangsters, perverts, misfits, and television repairmen. Your general health will continue to deteriorate, and you probably won't make it to the next full moon. Be of good cheer.

127. Executive Gift Suggestion

The format used by advertisers in popular magazines has also attracted the attention of the folk. The packaging of products and the use of such devices as snob appeal have been developed to a fine art. Nearly any product can be presented and promoted as an attractive, indispensable item. The following parody collected at Time/Life Books in New York City in 1975 illustrates some of these methods by advertising a novel gift item. A much more primitive rendering of a comparable theme, found in ISR, is also presented. For more on the rarely studied folklore of flatulence, see Legman's discussion in NLM, 858–90, Alfred Limbach, *Der Furz* (Köln: Argos Press, 1980), Colin Spencer and Chris Barlas, *Reports From Behind* (London: Enigma Books, 1984), and Bob Burton Brown, "Windy Words: A Glossary of Euphemisms for the Expulsion of Intestinal Gas," *Maledicta* 7 (1983): 149–54. See also Bob Burton Brown, *Common Scents: The First Book of Farts* (Gainesville: Moosebec Press, 1982).

EXECUTIVE GIFT SUGGESTION

FOR THE MAN WHO HAS EVERYTHING . . .

A TRAVELING ALARM CLOCK THAT BLOWS LIVE FARTS!

Originally developed for a wealthy, but deaf, industrialist from Athol, Mass. by the Auditory and Olfactory Perception Laboratory at M. I. T. This little gem of a clock can be set to emit a very loud and continuous fart (until cut off), accompanied by a powerful emission of chemically-compounded intestinal gas. (Clock also comes with warbler-effect feature, as well as volume and pitch controls).

The beauty of this unusual executive gift is that if the sound doesn't blow you out of bed in the morning the smell certainly will.

Ideal for the hard-of-hearing executive!

Ideal also for the traveling executive who gets homesick for his wife!

Ingenious gas insert canisters come in popular aromas:

- Chili con carne
- Cabbage
- Boston Baked Beans
- Brussell sprouts
- Gorgonzola
- Egg plant parmesan

WARNING: THE SURGEON GENERAL HAS CAUTIONED THAT EXECUTIVES SUBJECT TO NOSE—BLEEDING SHOULD BE AWAKENED BY OTHER MEANS.

SPECIAL CUSTOM FEATURE:

Custom-compressed live farts can be canistered and fortified at a charge of $25.00 per canister. All of this work is under the personal supervision of Col. Boris Blastyerassoff, formerly Chief of the Polish Chemical Warfare Service. Bonded representative will call at your residence to trap your own, or your wife's, live farts, and to make tape recordings.

Conversion to canister takes 2-3 weeks, except during hay-fever season when Col. Blastyerassoff returns to his native urals for relief.

EXECUGIFT INTERNATIONAL
290 Weed Street
New Canaan, Conn. 06840

Please rush me _____ farting clocks at $39.95 each.

Send also_____canisters of your _____ aroma at $10.00 each.

Please have bonded representative call for fart-trapping and recording session. Phone number_____

Name_____

Address_____

City_____
                    State   Zip

PORKY'S
Alarm Clock

Directions for Use — Just before going to sleep, instead of placing this candle in the candle stick, stick it in your ass up to the mark indicating the number of hours you wish to sleep, then lie on your face, light the candle and go to sleep.

NOTE—You must not fart in your sleep or you will blow out the candle.

| 8 | 7 | 6 | 5 | 4 | 3 | 2 | 1 |

128. A Compendium of Little-Known and Deservedly Obscure Baroque Ornaments

The following parody plays on the propensity of composers to employ musical directions to performers in either French or Italian. The following version, circulating in San Francisco in 1977, bears a credit line, "Compiled and fully annotated by Fred Palmer." If there is in fact a Fred Palmer, internal evidence would strongly suggest that he is an oboe player. Even nonmusicians should be able to appreciate most of the wit.

A COMPENDIUM OF LITTLE KNOWN AND DESERVEDLY OBSCURE BAROQUE ORNAMENTS

Compiled and fully annotated by

Fred Palmer

1. *Squeakment:*

This ornament is most commonly found in oboe literature. Beginning players discover it almost immediately.

2. *Thrill:*

This ornament cannot be admitted to the music unless the performer is over eighteen years of age or accompanied by a parent or guardian. It occurs at the climax of a piece.

3. *Waterment* (It. *gurglando*, Ger. *Wassernote*):

One of the most widely known baroque affects. It may have been inspired by the "Water Music" of Messrs. Händel and Telemann.

4. *Leaveitoutement:*

Written: Played:

This ornament is often found in modern editions of eighteenth century music.

5. *Messy di voce:*

This ornament is often added when the exact pitch of a note is in doubt.

6. *Spitment:*

Similar to the *Waterment* but with a short, sharp articulation.

7. *Castratement:*

A rather sterile ornament which should be cut off as soon as possible.

8. *Cripplement:*

This ornament is often replaced by the *tanglement* (see below).

9. *Tanglement:*

This ornament is often encountered in the oboe sonatas of Händel and Vivaldi.

10. *Goosement:*

Often found in third oboe parts.

11. *Schmaltzando:*

This ornament is a favorite with modern performers of baroque music.

12. *Scratchendo:*

Very common in Italian violin music.

13. *Tumblement:*

Very common in French violin music with triple stops.

14. *Squawkment:*

This is one of the most natural ornaments on the baroque oboe. Like the bird calls of the recorder, this ornament imitates the call of the crow, duck and blue jay.

15. *Gayment:*

This ornament is not heterogeneous since it is limited exclusively to the fagott.

16. *Pegment sans appuy:*

This ornament was very common in early viola da gamba music but was later suppressed by Gaspari.

17. *Apologytura:*

This is one of the oldest and most persistent ornaments in music. It can be traced all the way back to Gregorian Chant where it was known as the "mea culpa."

18. *Oberlin dissonance:*

This ornament occurs naturally when high and low pitch instruments play the same melody together.

19. *Sludgement:*

This articulation is often found in light, fast movements.

When You're up to Your Ass in Alligators . . .

20. *Fakement:*

Written: Played:

Oboe 1

Oboe 2

Oboe 3   Like the trill, this ornament is
obligatory—especially in pieces
written by composers who did not
Oboe 4   play the oboe.

Oboe 5

Oboe 6

21. *Belchment:*

This ornament is often used by wind players
—especially after a heavy meal.

22. *Clackment:*

This percussive ornament is often found on early woodwinds when keys
are brought into play. It produces an effect similar to artillery fire
and is best used in battle pieces.

23. *Approximatura:*

This ornament often occurs when several instruments
play the same written note.

24. *Quiverato:*

Although this ornament is a favorite of vocalists, it has
occasionally been used by string and wind players.

25. *Pour de vin:*

This flowing ornament is best taken after the last piece
on the program since it can mar an otherwise sober
performance if introduced too soon.

FINE?

129. How to Be Efficient with Fewer Violins

The notion of ornamentation may strike the nonmusician as an instance of unnecessary frills. Time and motion studies as part of the work of efficiency experts or management consultants would look askance at the redundancy and the apparent peculiar division of labor in most musical performances. In the following parody of a concert performance viewed from the perspective of an efficiency engineer, we see the dire effects of reducing art to principles of management science. This version was collected at the University of Texas Press in February 1976. It carried an elaborate headnote:

SOURCE: Baumol and Bowen, *The Performing Arts: The Economic Dilemma*, The Twentieth Century Fund, New York, 1966. Reprinted there from *Bulletin of the American Association of University Professors*, Autumn 1955. The first few paragraphs appeared previously in *Harper's Magazine*, June 1955; and it apparently had been published before that in the *O & M Bulletin*, house organ of His Majesty's Treasury of the Courts, by permission of the *Ministry of Transport Bulletin*.

In a version appearing in R. L. Weber, *A Random Walk in Science*, ed. E. Mendoza (New York: Crane, Russak & Co., 1973), p. 7 (reprinted from the NPL [National Physical Laboratory] *News* 236 [1969], 17), we find a different bracketed heading: "Organization and method research is carried out to improve the efficiency of working of groups of people. The following are extracts from a report by O & M after a visit to the Royal Festival Hall." In addition, the final two paragraphs of the text presented below are absent and in their place is:

The conductor agrees generally with these recommendations, but expresses the opinion that there might be some falling-off in box-office receipts. In that unlikely event it should be possible to close sections of the auditorium entirely, with a consequential saving of overhead expense—lighting, attendants, etc.

If the worst came to the worst, the whole thing could be abandoned and the public could go to the Albert Hall instead.

This version is nearly identical with the one that appeared in *Harper's Magazine* in 1955. That version is labeled an "Anonymous memorandum circulating in London, 1955." See "How to

When You're up to Your Ass in Alligators . . .

Be Efficient with Fewer Violins," *Harper's Magazine* 210, no. 1261 (June 1955): 31. A version, which appeared as one of the "Traveller's Tales" reported by Derek Davies in the *Far Eastern Economic Review* 95 (5) (1977): 17, uses a different premise. A company chairman who had been given tickets for a performance of Schubert's "Unfinished Symphony" was unable to attend. He passed the tickets to his work-study consultant. When the chairman later asked the consultant how he enjoyed the performance, he was handed the item as a memorandum. The concluding paragraph of the memorandum reads: "If Schubert had adopted such techniques, he may have been able to finish his Symphony after all."

HOW TO BE EFFICIENT WITH FEWER VIOLINS

The following is the report of a Work Study Engineer after a visit to a symphony concert at the Royal Festival Hall in London.

For considerable periods the four oboe players had nothing to do. The number should be reduced and the work spread more evenly over the whole of the concert, thus eliminating peaks of activity.

All the twelve violins were playing identical notes; this seems unnecessary duplication. The staff of this section should be drastically cut. If a larger volume of sound is required, it could be obtained by means of electronic apparatus.

Much effort was absorbed in the playing of the demi-semi-quavers; this seems to be an unnecessary refinement. It is recommended that all notes should be rounded off to the nearest semi-quaver. If this were done it would be possible to use trainees and lower-grade operatives more extensively.

There seems to be too much repetition of some musical passages. Scores should be drastically pruned. No useful purpose is served by repeating on the horns a passage which has already been handled by the strings. It is estimated that if all redundant passages could be eliminated, the whole concert time of 2 hours could be reduced to 20 minutes and there would be no need for an intermission.

It was noted that the pianist was not only carrying out most of his work by two-handed operations, but was also using both feet for pedal operations. Nevertheless, there were excessive reaches for some notes on the piano and it is possible that redesign of the keyboard to bring all notes within the normal working area would be of advantage to this operator. In many cases the operators were using one hand for holding the instrument, whereas the use of a fixture would have rendered the idle hand available for other work.

Obsolescence of equipment is another matter into which it is suggested further investigation could be made, as it was reputed in the program that the leading violinist's instrument was already several hundred years old. If normal depreciation schedules had been applied, the value of this instrument should have been reduced to zero and it is possible that purchase of more modern equipment could have been considered.

130. The Passing of the Backhouse

A folk poem, which has been in tradition for at least fifty years, describes an outhouse in nostalgic and sentimental terms. The poem is almost always attributed to James Whitcomb Riley. Whether he wrote it or not, the poem does parody his style and his general tendency to romanticize humble aspects of rural life. Scholars have vehemently denied the attribution to Riley. They of course could not help noticing the continued printing of the poem "in broadside, leaflet, and pamphlet form, under various titles: 'The Country Privy,' 'The Passing of the Old Back-House,' etc." According to the discussion by Anthony J. and Dorothy R. Russo, one of the printed versions contains the statement "An unpublished poem by James Whitcomb Riley found among his manuscripts after his death." However, no such manuscript has ever been found, and Riley's close friends and relatives said that he did not write the poem. No reference to the poem occurs in his correspondence. William Lyon Phelps, the distinguished editor of *The Letters of James Whitcomb Riley*, stated in 1943 that he had found no proof whatever that Riley had written the poem.

It is clear that we have another instance of written folklore— whether Riley composed the poem or not. Comparison of the versions (texts as well as titles) demonstrates the variation that is the hallmark of most authentic folklore. In the light of the lack of any concrete evidence, one may assume that the poem was not written by Riley but that it was a folk parody falsely attributed to Riley from its inception. In any case, authorship is rarely an issue in folklore. For the scholarly view of the attribution to Riley, see Anthony J. and Dorothy R. Russo, *A Bibliography of James Whitcomb Riley* (Indianapolis: Indiana Historical Society, 1944), p. 233. The version presented here was collected in Washington, D.C., in 1976.

The Passing of the Backhouse

When memory keeps me company and moves to smiles or tears,
A weather-beaten object looms through the mist of years.
Behind the house and barn it stood, a half mile or more,
And hurrying feet a path had made, straight to its swinging door.
Its architecture was a type of simple classic art,
But in the tragedy of life it played a leading part.
And oft the passing traveler drove slow, and heaved a sigh,
To see the modest hired girl slip out with glances shy.

We had our posey garden that the women loved so well,
I loved it, too, but better still I loved the stronger smell
That filled the evening breezes so full of homely cheer,
And told the night-o'ertaken tramp that human life was near.
On lazy August afternoons, it made a little bower
Delightful, where my grandsire sat and whiled away an hour.
For there the summer morning its very cares entwined,
And berry bushes reddened in the steaming soil behind.

All day fat spiders spun their webs to catch the buzzing flies
That flitted to and from the house, where Ma was baking pies.
And once a swarm of hornets bold, had built a palace there,
And stung my unsuspecting aunt—I must not tell you where.
Then father took a flaming pole—that was a happy day—
He nearly burned the building up, but the hornets left to stay.
When summer bloom began to fade and winter to carouse
We banked the little building with a heap of hemlock boughs.

But when the crust was on the snow and the sullen skies were
    gray,
In sooth the building was no place where one could wish to stay.
We did our duties promptly, there one purpose swayed the mind.
We tarried not, nor lingered long on what we left behind.
The torture of that icy seat would make a Spartan sob,

For needs must scrape the goose-flesh with a lacerating cob
That from a frost-encrusted nail, was suspended by a string—
For father was a frugal man and wasted not a thing.

When grandpa had to "go out back" and make his morning call,
We'd bundle up the dear old man with a muffler and a shawl,
I knew the hole on which he sat—'twas padded all around,
And once I dared to sit there—'twas all too wide I found.
My loins were all too little, and I jack-knifed there to stay,
They had to come and get me out, or I'd have passed away.
Then father said ambition was a thing that boys should shun,
And I just used the children's hole 'till childhood days were done.

And still I marvel at the craft that cut those holes so true,
The baby hole, and the slender hole that fitted Sister Sue;
That dear old country landmark, I tramped around a bit,
And in the lap of luxury my lot has been to sit.
But ere I die I'll eat the fruit of trees I robbed of yore,
Then seek the shanty where my name is carved upon the door.
I ween the old familiar smell will soothe my jaded soul,
I'm now a man, but none the less, I'll try the children's hole.

—James Whitcomb Riley.

131. The Night before Christmas

A popular parody in oral and copier tradition takes as its point of departure Clement Clarke Moore's classic "Twas the Night before Christmas." Moore composed his poem, originally entitled "The Visit of Saint Nicholas," for his children in 1822. One year later, Miss Harriet Butler, daughter of the rector of Saint Paul's Church in Troy, New York, visited Reverend Moore and saw the poem. She received permission to make a copy of it but she elected to send it anonymously to the editor of the *Troy Sentinel*. Moore was annoyed at the public appearance in a newspaper of a poem he had written for the amusement of children. The poem became popular but not until more than fifteen years later was Moore willing to admit he was its author. No doubt he thought that the poem was beneath the dignity of a professor of divinity at the Theological Seminary in New York. He had also taken liberties with the Saint Nicholas tradition, for the saint typically appeared on the eve of December 5, before the day of Saint Nicholas, December 6. Although Moore may not have invented the reindeer means of locomotion, he apparently did set the number at eight and he gave them their classical and German names: Dasher, Dancer, Prancer, Vixen, Comet, Cupid, Donner and Blitzen. (The curious admixture of names from different linguistic traditions is perhaps symbolic of the variety of names found in America.)

Moore might have been even more embarrassed had he had any idea of the parodies his poem would spawn. Among the parody traditions stemming from Moore's poems, by far the most common one depicts a depraved family and a dissolute Santa Claus. The sanctity of the family and of the Christmas tradition is lost in a farcical maze of obscene detail. The version presented below was collected in Alameda, California, in 1974. It is representative except that the title is usually "The Night before Christmas" rather than "Merry Christmas." Although it circulates by means of copier, it is also recited in oral tradition. A rare second version, collected in San Francisco in 1976, presents a crapulous Santa. (For another version of our first text, see Mac E. Barrick, "The Typescript Broadside," *Keystone Folklore Quarterly* 17 [1972]: 35–36. For an English text, see TCB, 170–71.)

MERRY CHRISTMAS

Twas the night before Xmas and all thru the house
The whole goddam family was drunk as a louse
Grandma and Grandpa were singing a song
And the kid was in bed a flogging his dong
Ma, home from the cat house, and me out of jail
Had just crawled into bed for a nice piece of tail
When out on the lawn, there arose such a clatter
I jumped out of bed to see what was the matter
Away to the window I flew like a flash
Threw open the shutters and fell on my ass
The moon on the crest of the new fallen snow
Gave a whore-house-like luster to the objects below
When what to my blood shot eyes should appear
But a rusty old sleigh and two mangy reindeer

With a little old driver a pounding his dick
I knew in a moment, it must be Saint Nick
Slower than snails his reindeer they came
He bitched and he swore as he called them by name
Now Dancer, now Prancer, up over the walls
Quick now goddam it, or I'll cut out your balls.
Then up to the roof he stumbled and fell
And came down the chimney like a bat out of hell
He staggered and stomped and went to the door
Tripped on his peter, and fell on the floor
I heard him exclaim, as he rode out of sight:
Piss on you all, this is a hell of a night.

THE NIGHT BEFORE CHRISTMAS

Twas the night before Xmas and all through the house
There were empties and butts, left around by some louse.
And the best quart I'd hid by the chimney with care
Had been swiped by some bum, who'd discovered it there.
My guests all had long since been poured in their beds
To wake in the morning with god awful heads.
My mouth, full of cotton, hung down on my lap
Because I was dying for one more nightcap.
Where thru the north window there came such a smell
I sprang to my feet to see what the hell.
And what to my wondering eyes should show up
But eight bloated reindeer, hitched to a beer truck
With a little old driver who looked like a hick
But I saw it was Santa, as tight as a tick.
Staggering onward, those eight reindeer came,
While he hiccoughed and belched as he called them by name:
"On Schenley! On Seagram! We ain't got all night,
You too, Haig and Haig, and you too Black and White"
"Scram up on the roof, get the hell off this wall,
Get going you dummies, we've got a long haul."
So up on the roof went the reindeer and truck
But a tree branch hit Santa before he could duck.
And then, in a twinkling I heard from above
A hell of a noise that was no cooing dove.
So I pulled in my head and I cocked a sharp ear,
Down the chimney he plunged, landing smack on his rear,

He was dressed up in furs, no cuffs on his pants
And the way the guy squirmed, well I guess he had ants.
He had pints and quarts in the sack on his back
And a breath that'al blow a freight train right off the track
He was chubby and plump and he tried to stand right
But he didn't fool me, he was high as a kite.
He spoke not a word, but went straight to work
And missed half the stockings, the plastered old jerk.
Then putting five fingers to the end of his nose,
He gave me the bird . . . up the chimney he rose.
He sprang for his truck at so hasty a pace
That he tripped on a gable and slid on his face.
But I heard him burp back when he passed out of sight.
"Merry Christmas, you rum-dums, now really get tight."

132. Di Tri Berrese

The use of pseudo-Italian dialect in particular is featured in several folktale parodies. To appreciate fully the cleverness of the following "Italian" version of "The Three Bears," one must read it aloud while trying to imitate the stereotype version of Italian-American pronunciation of English. It may be difficult for some on the first reading to recognize "No mugheggia" as "No mortgage" or "Fette Cienze" as "Fat Chance." This item, which has been collected coast to coast, also displays the usual variation. Sometimes the "bietenicche Berrese" (beatnik Bears) are "Italienne berrese" (Italian bears). Sometimes rather than being "rattefinghe" (ratfinks), the three bears are described as "sanima biggiest" or "sanimabicese" or "sonnibicese" (son of a bitch). In one version, collected in Orinda, California, in 1977, from an Italian-American, the final line refers to "Tammeniollo" (Tammany Hall) rather than "sittiolle" (City Hall).

The version presented here was read at a party in 1963 in Los Angeles. (For another version, see UFFC-TB, 135.) The tale being parodied is a popular one in the English-speaking world. It first appeared in print in 1837 in *The Doctor* by Robert Southey, according to folklorist K. M. Briggs, who suggests the tale may have had older oral antecedents. For some discussion of the tale, see

K. M. Briggs, "The Three Bears," *IV International Congress for Folk-Narrative Research in Athens*, ed. Georgios A. Megas, *Laographia* 22 (1965): 53–57. For other discussions, see E. D. Phillips, "The Three Bears," *Man* 54 (1954): 123; Mary I. Shamburger and Vera R. Lachmann, "Southey and the Three Bears," *Journal of American Folklore* 59 (1946): 400–403; Eugene A. Hammel, *The Myth of Structural Analysis: Lévi-Strauss and the Three Bears*. Addison-Wesley Module in Anthropology 25 (1972); and Alan C. Elms, "'The Three Bears': Four Interpretations," *Journal of American Folklore* 90 (1977): 257–73.

DI TRI BERRESE

(di'sse libretto ise for dos iu laicho tu follow di spiccher wail ise spicche)

Uans appona taim uas tri berres; mamma berre, pappa berre, a bebi berre. Live inne contri nire foresta. NAISE AUS. NO mugheggia. Uanno dei, pappa, mamma e beibe go tooda bice, onie, furghette locche di doore. Bai enne bai commese Goldilocchese. Sci garra nattinghe tudu batto meiche troble. Sci puschie olle fudde daon di maute; no live somme. Dan sci gos appesterrese enne slipse in olle di beddse.
LEISI SLOBBE!
Bai enne bai commese omme di tri berrese, olle sonnebronde enne sand inne scius. Dei garra no fudde; dei garra no beddse. En wara dei goine due tu Goldilocchese? Tro erre inne strit? Colle pulissemenne?
FETTE CIENZE!
Dei uas bietenicche Berrese, enne dei slippe onna floore. Goldilocchese stei derre tree dase; itte aute ausenomme en giusta bicose dei asche erro tu meiche di beddse, sci sei "GO TU ELLE," enne runne omme criane to erre mamma, tellen erre uat rattefinghe di tri berrese uor. Uatsiuse? Uara iu goine due—Go compliene sittiolle?

When You're up to Your Ass in Alligators . . .

133. Prinderella and the Cince

A parody technique involving typically some type of spooner-istic interchange is demonstrated in the various versions of Cin-derella parodies. Although these parodies are often written, they are normally delivered orally from memory. Their performance requires much verbal skill. To show the variation possible, we have included three versions. The first was reported in Chicago about 1956; the second from the University of Kentucky in 1971, and the third from San Francisco in 1973. Another version, often performed by Archie Campbell on the "Hee Haw" television show, appeared in print. See Archie Campbell, "Rindercella," *Hee Haw* 1, no. 1 (May 1970): 17.

The tale parodied is Cinderella, Aarne-Thompson tale type 510A. A favorite fairy tale among girls, it is no surprise that much of the major scholarship has been by female folklorists. One of the first comparative studies of any folktale was Marian R. Cox's *Cinderella* (London: David Nutt, 1893). A more recent mono-graph is Anna Birgitta Rooth's *The Cinderella Cycle* (Lund: C. W. K. Gleerup, 1951). For a substantial sampling of the schol-arship devoted to Cinderella, see Alan Dundes, ed., *Cinderella: A Folklore Casebook* (New York: Garland, 1982).

Prinderella and the Cince

Here is a story that will make your clesh freep. It will give you poose gimples. Just think of a poor little glip of a sirl, pery vretty. Just because she has two sisty uglers she has to flop the moor, crinkle the shovers out of the stichen kove, and do all the other shasty nores, while her slomely histers go to a drancy bess-fall. Now isn't that a shirty dame?

To make a long shory stort, this yapless houngster was flop-ping the kitchen moor one day, when who should appear but her gairy fodmother. Beeling very fadly for this wetty praife, she happed her clans, said a couple of wagic mords, and in the esh of a flyebrow Cinderella was transformed into a bravishing reauty. And out on the sturb cone stood a magnificent colden goach, made of a pipe yellow rumpkin. Cinderella thanked her gairy fodmother from the hottom of her beart, bimed a cloard, the driver whracked his cip, and they were off in a doud of clust. Soon they came to a castleful wonder, where a prandsome hince was possing a tarty for the teople of the pound. She alighted, hanked her droperchief, and out came the prince who was teeping at her all the pime from a widden hindow.

Well, the nince went pruts over the povely lincess. But at the moke of stridnight, Scramderella suddenly Cind. As she went running down the long staircase, she slicked off one of her glass kippers, and the pounce princed upon it with eaming glyes.

The next day he tried all over the town to find the lainty dady whose foot fitted the slipper. The only foot that fitted was none other than our lady leading. And so she parried the mince, and they all lived happily after everwards.

Prinderella and the Cince

Twonce upon a wime, there was a gritty little pirl named Prinderella who lived with her two sugly isters her sticked weptmother (who made her pine the shots and shans and do all the other wirty dirk around the house.) Wasn't that a shirty dame?

One day the Ping issued a kroclamation saying that all geligible irls were impited to the valace for a drancy fess ball. The two sugly isters and the sticked weptmother were oing, but Prinderella couldn't go because she didn't have a drancy fess. All she had was an old rirty dag which fidn't dit! Wasn't *that* a shirty dame?

But, along came Prinderella's Gairie Fodmother who changed a cumpkin into a peach and hice into morses, and sent Prinderella off to the palace saying, "Don't forget to come home at the moke of stridnight!"

So, at the moke of stridnight, Prinderella ran down the stalace peps, but on the bottom pep, she slopped her dripper. Wasn't that a shirty dame?!

Well, the next day, the Ping issued another kroclamation saying that all geligible irls were to sly on the lost tripper. The two sugly isters and the sticked weptmother slied on the tripper, but it fidn't dit. Prinderella slied on the tripper and it fid dit! So, Prinderella and the Cince mot garried and hived lappily ever after.

!!!!!!!!!!!!!!!!!!!!!!

End of tairy fale!

The Story of Prinderella and The Cince

Tonce upon a wime, there gived a little irl named Prinderella. Prinderella's dother had mied, and her mather had faried again, leaving poor Prinderella to live with her two sisty uglers and her wicked mepstother. They treated Prinderella something awful. They made her wean the clindows, pine the shots and shans, flop the kitchen moors, and do all the shirty dores around the house.

Done way, the ping sent out a croclamation throughout the land that all the geligible irls were invited to attend a drancy fess ball in honor of the cince, who had just become of age.

On the dight of the nance, the wicked mepstother and the two sisty uglers dressed up in their drancy fesses and ove droff to the palace, leaving poor Prinderella at home. She couldn't go because she had no drancy fess. All she had were dirty dags so she cat down and scried. But suddenly there appeared her mairy fodgother, who said, "Crop stying, Prinderella. You gal toe shoo." And in the eyeling of a twink, she changed the cumpkin to a poach, the drog into a diver and Prinderella's dirty dags into a drancy fess. And as Prinderella ove droff toward the palace, her mairy fodgother cried after her: "Remember, my dear, at the first moke of stridnight you must return for then all shall be as before."

So Prinderella went to the nance and she nanced all dight with the cince. But at the first moke of stridnight, she rushed down the stalace peps, and on the stottom tep, she slopped her dripper.

The cince, running behind Prinderella, picked up the dripper and ran after her. But she was gone, and all was as before.

The dext nay, the ping sent out another croclamation that all the geligible irls who had attended the drancy fess ball were to try on the dripper to see who it fit. When the ping's messenger arrived at the house of the wicked mepstother and the two sisty uglers, the old bats rocked Prinderella in her loom. They tried on the dripper, and of course it didn't fit. Prinderella, meanwhile, escaped from her rocked loom, stood on the stop tep, and cried: "Let me try on the dripper."

Well, she tried it on, and it fit. So Prinderella and the cince were married the dame say and lived happily afterever ward.

134. The Modern Little Red Hen

Stories written like traditional folktales but not passed on from person to person fail to qualify as bona fide folklore. Children's literature includes both authentic folktales and literary efforts by known authors. Occasionally, literary tales succeeded in achieving the same currency and esthetic appeal as folktales. Yet these literary tales for all their merit do not exist with variation in more than one time and place. The text of the story remains almost unchanged over the years.

One classic of children's literature is the story of the little red hen. The story is not indexed in Antti Aarne and Stith Thompson, *The Types of the Folktale*, 2d rev. FFC 184 (Helsinki: Academia Scientiarum Fennica, 1961) and so one would assume that it is not a folktale. On the other hand, there are many editions or versions of the tale in print (as a children's book) by many authors. In any case, whether a folktale or a literary imitation, this formula tale has achieved the necessary status to warrant its being the basis for parody. In the original parable, a hen seeks help in planting and harvesting a crop on a farm. All the animals in turn refuse to assist the little red hen. She does all the work herself. When the other animals see the results of her labor, they ask to share in the bounty. She replies using the same phrase they had used earlier in declining to assist her. The story clearly exemplifies the Puritan work ethic and celebrates the rewards of capitalistic free enterprise.

The parody, entitled variously "A Modern Fable" and "The Little Red Hen (Revisited)," has been attributed to "Doug Smith, a British Columbia writer" and to "William P. Drake, president of the Penwalt Corporation," who supposedly composed and read it at the annual meeting of his company in 1975. (Some versions that have appeared in company and organization newsletters indicate the author is not known.) The modern version of the tale complains about government interference with the free enterprise system. From this point of view, the redistribution of wealth through taxation and the attempt to build a welfare state destroy the incentive necessary to make the capitalistic system work properly. The version presented here circulated in Portland, Oregon, in 1977.

When You're up to Your Ass in Alligators . . .

A MODERN FABLE

Once upon a time, there was a little red hen who scratched about and uncovered some grains of wheat. She called her neighbors and said, "If we plant this wheat, we will have bread to eat. Who will help me plant it?"

"Not I," said the cow.

"Not I," said the duck.

"Not I," said the goose.

"Then I will," said the little red hen. And she did. The wheat grew tall and ripened into golden grain. "Who will help me reap my wheat?" asked the little red hen.

"Not I," said the duck.

"Out of my classification," said the pig.

"I'd lose my seniority," said the cow.

"I'd lose my unemployment insurance," said the goose.

"Then I will," said the little red hen, and she did. At last it came time to bake the bread.

"That's overtime for me," said the cow.

"I'm a dropout and never learned how," said the duck.

"I'd lose my welfare benefits," said the pig.

"If I'm the only helper, that's discrimination," said the goose.

"Then I will," said the little hen. She baked five loaves and held them up for her neighbors to see. They all wanted some and demanded a share. But the little red hen said, "No, I can eat the five loaves myself."

"Excess Profits!" cried the cow.

"Capitalist leech!" screamed the duck.

"Equal rights!" yelled the goose. And they painted "Unfair" picket signs and marched around the little red hen, shouting obscenities.

When the government agent came, he said, "You must not be greedy, little red hen."

"But I earned the bread," said the little red hen.

"Exactly," said the agent. "That is the wonderful free enterprise system. Anybody in the barnyard can earn as much as he wants. But under our modern government regulations, the productive workers must divide their product with the idle."

And they lived happily ever after, including the little red hen, who smiled and clucked, "I am grateful. I am grateful."

But her neighbors wondered why she never baked any more bread.

In earlier versions (1973) several differences are apparent. The picketers sing "We Shall Overcome" rather than shout obscenities. A farmer (rather than a government agent) advises: "You must not be greedy, little Red Hen. Look at the oppressed cow. Look at the disadvantaged duck. Look at the underprivileged pig. Look at the less fortunate goose. You are guilty of making second-class citizens of them." After the little red hen objects that she earned the bread, the farmer continues, "That is the wonderful free enterprise system; anybody in the barnyard can earn as much as he wants. You should be happy to have this freedom. In other barnyards, you'd have to give all five loaves to the farmer. Here you give four loaves to your suffering neighbors."

135. Inspiration for the Unhappy

Another pseudofable found coast to coast concerns the misadventures of a sparrow who unwisely delayed his flight south for the winter. The convention of using animal characters to portray human foibles is an ancient one. Animal fables are a major type of the general fable form. Typically fables end with a moral. In this example, the American (and western) penchant for the number three has resulted in no fewer than three morals. For a discussion of the fable genre, see Erwin Leibfried, *Fabel* (Stuttgart: J. B. Metzlersche Verlagsbuchhandlung, 1967) or Ben Edwin Perry's introduction to *Babrius and Phaedrus* (Cambridge: Harvard University Press, 1975) or the same author's "Fable," *Studium Generale* 12 (1959): 17–37. See also Pack Carnes, *Fable Scholarship: An Annotated Bibliography* (New York: Garland, 1985). For more on the number three, see Alan Dundes, "The Number Three in American Culture," in *Every Man His Way* (Englewood Cliffs: Prentice-Hall, 1968), pp. 401–24.

The fable parody of the sparrow circulates with titles as long as "If You Are At All Unhappy with Your Lot in Life, This Story May Inspire You" or as short as "If You Are Unhappy." The title "Inspiration for the Unhappy" is by far the most common for this extremely popular tale. The version presented here was obtained in 1969 from the desk of a hospital administrator in San Francisco. Of special interest is the literalization in the fable of several

When You're up to Your Ass in Alligators . . .

well-known metaphors involving feces. (For two other versions, see UFFC-TB, 137–38.)

INSPIRATION FOR THE UNHAPPY

Once upon a time there was a little sparrow who hated to fly south for the winter. He dreaded the thought of leaving his home so much that he decided he would delay the journey until the last possible moment.

After bidding farewell to all his sparrow friends, he went back to his nest and stayed for an additional four weeks. Finally, the weather turned so bitterly cold that he could delay no longer. As the little sparrow took off and started to fly south, it began to rain. In a short time, ice began to form on his little wings. Almost dead from cold and exhaustion, he fell to the earth in a barnyard. As he was breathing what he thought was his last breath, a horse walked out of the barn and proceeded to cover the little bird with fertilizer. At first the sparrow could think of nothing except that this was a terrible way to die. But as the fertilizer started to sink into his feathers, it warmed him and life began to return to his body. He also found that he had enough room to breathe. Suddenly the little sparrow was so happy that he started to sing.

At that moment a large cat came into the barnyard and, hearing the chirping of the little bird, began digging into the pile of fertilizer to find out where the sound was coming from. The cat finally uncovered the bird and ate him.

NOW, THIS STORY CONTAINS <u>THREE</u> MORALS:
1. Not everyone who shits on you is your enemy.
2. Not everyone who takes shit off you is your friend.
3. When you are warm and comfortable, even if it is in a pile of shit, <u>KEEP YOUR MOUTH SHUT</u>.

136. Obituary

It might be hard for some to imagine how an obituary could be a vehicle for humor. And yet, part of the ritual in wakes often includes riotous humor. Perhaps it is only in humor that the grim reality of death can be faced. If there is any truth to the idea that the greater the anxiety, the greater the need for humor about the source of that anxiety, one should not be surprised by the content of the following obituary parody.

This parody contains a litany of Italian-American stereotypes: supposed occupational preferences, large families, and the loyalties to ethnic neighborhood associations. It includes references to the practice of some churches in raising revenues through a form of gambling, namely bingo games, and to the criminal element of the Mafia, or "family." The version presented here was collected in Hastings-on-Hudson, New York, in 1976. In other versions from New York City, Buffalo, and Los Altos, California, there are slight variations. For example, these versions do not include the "Special to the *New York Times*" heading, the final sentence referring to the family, or the journalistic symbol "30," meaning originally in telegraphy the end of a message, but in journalism signifying the end of a newspaper article. (Thirty, apparently, was occasionally used as a metaphor for death itself. See Harold Wentworth and Stuart Berg Flexner, *Dictionary of American Slang* [New York: Thomas Y. Crowell, 1967], p. 542.) On the other hand, all these versions agree with one another that the name of the target of the knife throwing was Inadverto Castrata and that the name of the church was St. Bastardo.

Special to the *New York Times*, 21 March 1976

Obituary

Porcofacio Inscrupulata, contractor, of 100 Grotto Blvd., South Beach, Staten Island, died yesterday of injuries received in the collapse of a building he was inspecting prior to sale at public auction. Mr. Inscrupulata was 62.

Born in Mt. Marrone, Sicily, Inscrupulata was brought to this country at the age of eleven by his parents, Regurgito and Nauseata Inscrupulata. Prior to his untimely death, Inscrupulata was president of the Neglegente Construction Co. which he founded with his late brother, Devio. Before his association with the Neg-

When You're up to Your Ass in Alligators . . .

legente company, Mr. Inscrupulata was an executive with the Profumo Cesspool Cleaning and Catering Corporation.

He is survived by his wife, Inconsolata, their sons, Retardo, Cretino, and Imbecilio, daughters, Overia, Fallopia and Clitoria; two sisters, Mrs. Hysteria Psychosi and Mrs. Mammeria Pendulosa; and a brother, Prolifico Fornicato, and fourteen grandchildren, all of the Grotto Blvd. address.

Active for many years in community affairs, Mr. Inscrupulata was a member of the Sons of Sicily Sharpshooters Society and the Il Duce Theology and Bocce Club, the Insanitarios Pizzeria bowling team and also served as president of the South Beach Pink Flamingo Lawn and Garden Alliance. Until recently he appeared in local carnivals and nightclubs performing a knife-throwing act with his friend, the late Inadverto Decapitata.

The Rev. Celibato Infortunato of St. Carnivalo's R.C. Church will offer a Solemn High Requiem Bingo Game on Wednesday. Interment will be in the Arriverderci Roma Memorial Park. Funeral arrangements will be handled through the Rigori-Mortisco Funeral Parlor and Excavating Co. The funeral will be private and open only to members of the "family."

–30–

137. Writer's Block

If death can be a subject for parody, no topic is immune from the attention of parodists. Some academics take themselves seriously, so it really is no surprise to learn that the academic enterprise can inspire humor. One of the principal paths to success in the academic world lies in publication. "Publish or Perish" is the pertinent form of the more basic "Do or Die" proverb (also given in more vernacular fashion as "Shit or get off the pot"). The would-be academic who finds himself unable to write learned articles and monographs has little hope of attaining a coveted post at a prestigious college or university.

In the following text collected in Berkeley in 1981, we find many of the typical signs of life in the "ivory tower." One must write a paper, present it at a national convention to impress peers, submit it to a major journal in the field, which sends it for review to determine whether it is worthy of publication, and finally, if the paper is published, send reprints to interested and influential colleagues. Any subject can be the focus of a serious, worthwhile study, and even negative results may be deemed publishable. It is in this light that the ingenious paper on an unsuccessful treatment of writer's block should be read. Implicit also is the idea that psychologists, who are supposedly experts in behavior, often cannot solve their own problems. This item really appeared in the *Journal of Applied Behavior Analysis* in 1974. What is significant is that it circulates by means of copy machine throughout the country.

JOURNAL OF APPLIED BEHAVIOR ANALYSIS 1974, 7, 497 NUMBER 3 (FALL 1974)

THE UNSUCCESSFUL SELF-TREATMENT OF
A CASE OF "WRITER'S BLOCK"[1]

DENNIS UPPER

VETERANS ADMINISTRATION HOSPITAL, BROCKTON, MASSACHUSETTS

REFERENCES

---

[1]Portions of this paper were not presented at the 81st Annual American Psychological Association Convention, Montreal, Canada, August 30, 1973. Reprints may be obtained from Dennis Upper, Behavior Therapy Unit, Veterans Administration Hospital, Brockton, Massachusetts 02401.

Received 25 October 1973.
(Published without revision.)

COMMENTS BY REVIEWER A

I have studied this manuscript very carefully with lemon juice and X-rays and have not detected a single flaw in either design or writing style. I suggest it be published without revision. Clearly it is the most concise manuscript I have ever seen—yet it contains sufficient detail to allow other investigators to replicate Dr. Upper's failure. In comparison with the other manuscripts I get from you containing all that complicated detail, this one was a pleasure to examine. Surely we can find a place for this paper in the Journal—perhaps on the edge of a blank page.

138. New Classes in Continuing Education

Higher education has attempted to become more relevant to larger groups of the population, and it has tried to accomplish this through curriculum revision. In university extension courses that seek students in weekend or evening time periods, there has been an increasing effort to offer intriguing if not overly trendy courses to entice enough students to make the extension program financially self-supporting. Many of these innovative, experimental extension courses would probably not be approved by the academic committees governing the content of regular college and university courses. The following text, collected in Berkeley in 1982, comments on some of the more popular themes in such extension courses. (For another version, see YD, 20.)

INTEROFFICE CORRESPONDENCE

To   All Interested Employees   6-16-82

From   Office of Continuing Education

Subject Employee Development, 1982 Class Offerings

BELOW IS A PARTIAL LIST OF THE CLASSES BEING OFFERED TO ALL EMPLOYEES BEGINNING FALL, 1982

SELF IMPROVEMENT

Creative Suffering
Overcoming Peace of Mind
Guilt Without Sex
Ego Gratification Through Violence
Creative Depression
Whine Your Way to Alienation
How to Overcome Self-Doubt Through Pretense and Ostentation
A New Drug to Enhance Your Social Life
The Art of Indecision

BUSINESS AND CAREER

Money Can Make You Rich
I Made $100 in Real Estate
Career Opportunities In El Salvador
How to Profit From Your Own Body
The Underachiever's Guide to Very Small Business Opportunities
Looter's Guide to America's Cities
Learning the Proper Way to Harass
Growing Grass for Fun and Profit

HEALTH & FITNESS

Creative Tooth Decay
Exorcism and Acne
The Joys of Hypochondria
High Fiber Sex
Biofeedback and How to Stop It
Skate Yourself to Regularity
Understanding Nudity
Tap Dance Your Way to Social Ridicule
Optimum Body Functions

CRAFTS

Self-Actualization Through Macramé
How to Draw Genitalia
Needlecraft for Junkies
Bonsai Your Pet
Gifts for the Senile

HOME ECONOMICS

How You Can Convert Your Family Room into a Garage
What To Do With Your Conversation Piece
1001 Other Uses for Your Vacuum Cleaner
Burglarproof Your Home with Concrete
The Repair and Maintenance of Your Virginity
How to Convert a Wheelchair into a Dune Buggy
Christianity and the Art of RV Maintenance

Conclusions

Having presented a sample of the rich, diverse materials circulating in offices throughout the United States, we would like to make a few observations. First, these materials manifest multiple existence in time and space. As a result, there are many versions of individual items and these versions show the kinds of variation encountered in folkloristic phenomena everywhere. Accordingly, it is hard to understand the grounds on which anyone could argue that these materials are not traditional.

While there are some old-fashioned folklorists who continue to mistakenly limit their conception of "folk" to illiterate rural peasants, more and more twentieth-century folklorists have come to realize that there are many different types of folk groups, each of which has its own distinctive folklore. Among these folk groups must be included office workers, and a major component of office-worker folklore consists of copier folklore of the kind contained in this volume. Moreover, the existence of analogous, parallel texts in other countries, such as Ecuador, England, France, and Germany, suggests that many of the items reported here enjoy international distribution. As copier-machine technology spreads around the world, one may anticipate that copier folklore will follow in its wake. Whenever offices abound and bureaucracy flourishes, one will find copier folklore aplenty.

It is a commonplace of conventional wisdom among folklorists that technology kills folklore. The reasoning is that people will listen to radios, watch television, and attend movies rather than participate in traditional ballad-singing and tale-telling sessions. This may or may not be true. But one thing is certain, and that is that copier machines, surely an example of technology, are largely responsible for the rapid dissemination of copier folklore.

Indeed, we observe that technology itself (cf. the Italian [Polish] Calculator or "System Been Down Long?") has become the subject of modern urban folklore. This should once and for all put to rest the mistaken and oversimplified notion that technology kills folklore. Some traditional folklore may be on the wane, but technology, as this volume demonstrates conclusively, creates a folklore of its own.

Although folklorists have tacitly admitted that not all folklore is orally transmitted when they study such traditional forms as epitaphs, autograph-book verse, or bathroom-wall verse (latrinalia), they have been reluctant to consider the copier folklore reported in this volume as bona fide folklore. One looks in vain in major anthologies of American folklore for such materials. Similarly, one finds no mention of such copier folklore in the pages of the *Journal of American Folklore*, published continuously since 1888.

It is our hope that the publication of this collection of additional examples of copier folklore will encourage future folklorists as well as members of other disciplines to examine such materials. This material reflects the basic underlying anxieties and concerns of modern urban folk just as ballads and myths reflect the ideology and worldview of peoples in the past. On the few occasions when scholars have considered the materials in this volume, for example, the "B. Franklin Letter" or "The Passing of the Backhouse" or the "Regulation on the Sale of Cabbages," they failed to realize they were dealing with traditional folklore. The items were deemed instead to be hoaxes or frauds purposely perpetrated on an unwitting public. If the materials were discussed at all, it was only in derogatory terms. Ignored by folklorists and belittled by literary scholars, these neglected items have nevertheless continued to thrive among the folk. Some of the items have obviously originated relatively recently (e.g., the "Simplified 1040"), but many go back fifty or one hundred years or more. (In earlier times, the items had to be laboriously copied by hand or else typed.) Given the age of many of the items, it is truly surprising that so many of the items in this collection are appearing in published form for the first time.

Some may ask why these materials should be published at all. They may consider them to be offensive, trivial, and beneath the dignity of genteel educated people. Our point is that these materials exist whether all people like them or not. But more important, these materials provide windows affording a unique view of the innermost workings of American society. They demonstrate how Americans mask with humor their anxieties about sexual and ethnic identity, big government, complex technology, succeeding in business and marriage, and a host of other topics. When one thinks how prized are the fragments of mundane written texts from Sumer and other ancient civilizations for students of those cultures, one can only wonder at the consistent disregard of the materials in this volume by students of contemporary American culture. These materials are literally available for the asking and have been so for decades.

Many of the most significant themes of American culture—rugged individualism, racism, sexism—are all to be found displayed in this volume. The individual's constant struggle to maintain his equilibrium and identity in the face of increasingly large bureaucracies—big business and big government—is surely a major theme. The inevitable disparity between the ideal world and the real world is another. In a way, this volume of urban folklore from the paperwork empire may be said to be concerned with coping, coping with all the problems and petty annoyances of day-to-day living ranging from trying to find a parking place to registering a complaint when the system fails.

The fact that these traditional coping mechanisms contain humor should come as no surprise. For humor is often the only recourse in a difficult, anxiety-producing situation. The reader is urged not to be misled by the humor, however. It is, after all, only the most serious matters which can form the basis of humor. In a way, one could reasonably argue that the greater the laughter, the greater the problem which provoked the laughter. Beneath the mask of comedy often lies the face of tragedy. To the extent that we are confronted with an ever-increasing, bewildering series of forms, instructions, and memoranda to fill out and obey, we shall continue to need parodies of these devilish instruments of bureaucracy to retain our composure and sense of humor. No folklore exists unless there is a need for that folklore. So the existence of copier folklore must answer such a need. We suggest that the need might be for a measure of sanity in what sometimes appears to be an insane world.

Some might speculate that the presentation of a collection such as this volume might adversely affect the tradition's vitality. Might not the book supplant the need to make copies? It is true that one informant told us he was so intrigued with some of the items contained in UF that he copied them for his friends. But this means only that materials that were traditional to begin with are being further circulated. Furthermore, the number of persons likely to read this collection is but a miniscule part of all those people who participate in the tradition itself. The publication of jokebooks or songbooks does not inhibit the telling of jokes or the singing of songs by performers. It is possible that the materials in this volume may be different because they are written rather than oral, but we, frankly, doubt that the publication of this collection will in any way affect the vitality of the tradition. Variation will continue to occur in accordance with local conditions, and entirely new items will certainly appear.

Each of the items in this volume represents a separate instance of folk creativity. Many deserve intensive and extensive study. All remind us that one need not travel to the far ends of the earth to find folklore. Folklore lives in our own backyard. We can walk to the nearest office and chances are that we will find still more urban folklore from the paperwork empire.

Alan Dundes is professor of anthropology and folklore at the University of California, Berkeley. He holds an M.A.T. degree from Yale University and a Ph.D. in folklore from Indiana University. Widely published, Professor Dundes' works include *The Morphology of North American Indian Folktales* and *Life Is Like a Chicken Coop Ladder.* He has edited *The Study of Folklore* and *Mother Wit from the Laughing Barrel* and co-edited *The Wandering Jew.* He has also written numerous articles for scholarly journals.

Carl R. Pagter is a practicing attorney in California. He is currently vice president, secretary, and general counsel of Kaiser Cement Corporation in Oakland, California. He leads an old-time string band, Country Ham, that has performed nationally and has recorded ten long-playing record albums on the Vetco label. He and Professor Dundes collaborated on *Urban Folklore from the Paperwork Empire.* This volume is their second effort.

The manuscript was edited by Thomas Seller. The book was designed by Elizabeth Hanson. The typeface for the text is Trump.

Manufactured in the United States of America.